Arts & International Affairs

Volume 2, Issue 1

Winter 2017: "Performing Culture"

Edited by J. P. Singh

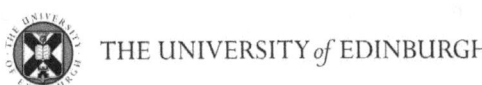

THE UNIVERSITY *of* EDINBURGH

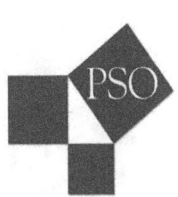

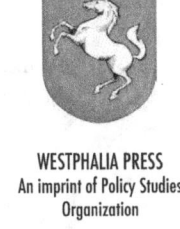

WESTPHALIA PRESS
An imprint of Policy Studies
Organization

Volume 2, Number 1 of Arts and International Affairs
All Rights Reserved © 2016 by Policy Studies Organization

Westphalia Press
An imprint of Policy Studies Organization
1527 New Hampshire Ave., NW
Washington, D.C. 20036
info@ipsonet.org

ISBN-10: 1-63391-511-5
ISBN-13: 978-1-63391-511-4

Cover design by Jeffrey Barnes:
jbarnesbook.design

Daniel Gutierrez-Sandoval, Executive Director
PSO and Westphalia Press

Updated material and comments on this edition
can be found at the Westphalia Press website:
www.westphaliapress.org

Table of Contents

Table of Contents

Theme 3: Performance + Heritage

Note on Journal Format

Arts & International Affairs features three types of articles: scholarly 'Longform' essays; shorter essays known as 'Brushstrokes'; and 'Multimedia', which are written essays with a focus on video, images and audio. Contributions are grouped into thematic sections.

University of Edinburgh *AIA* Advisory Board

The Institute for International Cultural Relations

The IICR was established in 2013 and is today situated in the School of Social and Political Science in the College of Arts, Humanities and Social Science. The IICR acts as a catalyst for interdisciplinary scholarship across the whole University, and as a bridge to practice. It also aims to connect with an internationally and inter-culturally diverse array of real-world communities, to help them face the many practical challenges they confront today.

Direct engagement and partnerships with external decision-maker, policy and practitioner communities are a unique strength of the IICR's educational and research programmes.

This vision is summarised by the objective of the IICR to be both applied in focus and global in reach. This vision is reflected in the commitment of the IICR community to expand and deepen our connections to decision-maker, policy and practitioner communities across the planet. As part of the global objective, the IICR aims to grow into an international educational ambassador for excellence in innovation and leadership on the interfaces among arts, humanities, social sciences and public policy. A priority for the IICR is to expand the impact of our expertise and research to a global audience through interdisciplinary and methodological rigor.

Performing Culture

J.P. Singh

J.P. Singh is Professor and Chair of Culture and Political Economy at The University of Edinburgh. He is Director of the Institute for International Cultural Relations, The University of Edinburgh.

Culture, replete with ritual, symbols and practices, is a performance.

Culture provides the historical and mimetic links all of us as actors need to re-present familiar and disruptive tropes to our audiences – the outsider and insider, celebration and violence, comfort and catharsis. It is in this interplay between actor and audience that the 'we' of culture makes it performative storytelling with recognizable, if not new, cues embedded in the artwork.

This performative aspect of culture might account for the bind between culture and Culture: the anthropological way of life culture and the culture of arts. In the call to prayer, lighting of candles, batteries playing at a carnival, or the sound of bagpipes in Scotland, cultural performances provide comfort through their execution. However, one person's affirming familiarity may be the other's strangeness. Collectively, we turn to the arts to witness interpretations of this alienation amid a sense of belonging; to understand it and make sense of it. It must a self-centered conceit then that storytelling too often narrates resolutions with a happy ending.

There are innumerable tropes and parables that creative works engage with, but stories of cultural interactions primarily are that of the familiar clashing with the unfamiliar. Edward Said's Orientalism (1978) reveals a world that the Occident found to be its veritable 'other'. The book has its devout followers and critics, but its central insights are confirmed through elementary sociology. Berger and Luckmann's *The Social Construction of Reality* (1966) enumerates the production of social meanings and their acceptance and institutionalization through language, censors ('reality checks'), and reification through everyday experience. Erving Goffman's *The Presentation of Self in Everyday Life* (1959) speaks to the disruptions in narrative cues for travelers. "Reports by Western traveler are filled with instances in which their dramaturgical sense was offended or surprised."

The reality of culture's fictions might well be that narratives are as much about anxiety as they are about the familiar. In a globalized world, otherness is bound to displace familiarity. We can see that multicultural interactions – facilitated in part by YouTube's 1 billion users in 88 countries and Facebook's 1.8 billion users –breed cultural anxiety. Audiences ill-equipped to venture outside the confines of the familiar may find it difficult, if not self-defeating, to derive comfort from performance without the assistance of tranquilizers, metaphorically speaking.

In times of great cultural anxiety, one person's new resolution will be countered with another's reactionary proposal. Take war monuments: the "gabbro" black marble-like Vietnam Veterans Memorial in Washington, DC lists names of 58,000 dead service members. It provides a somber and reflective moment about a drawn-out war fought thousands of miles away in the name of liberal democracy. Nearby, the World War II Memorial, completed in 2004, eulogizes heroism in war unequivocally with its 4 triumphal arches and 56 granite pillars mounted with laurel wreaths.

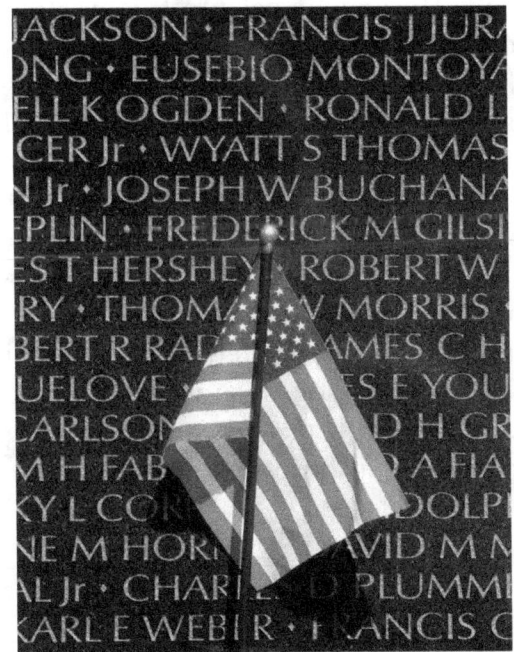

Vietnam Memorial, Washington DC

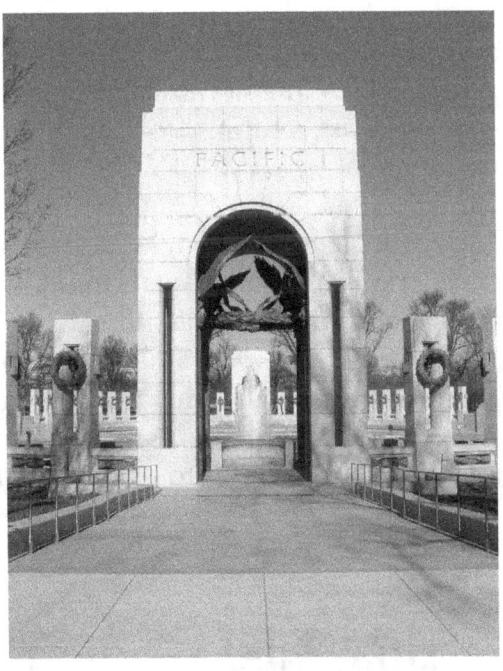

World War II Memorial, Washington DC

Bani Abidi's sound installation, "Memorial to Lost Words", featured at the 2016 Edinburgh Art Festival, is an 'anti-monumental' work that memorializes but also reorients. One hundred years after that first great war, Abidi replays the words Indian soldiers wrote in letters to their families during World War I alongside the counter narration of Punjabi ballads from women. The juxtaposed audio presents the centenary of World War I in context of colonialism and empire in a deeply personal way. Its affect evokes the residual legacy of British rule, making the old new to a modern audience.

Our theme for this issue, "Performing Culture", takes its cues from the art of dialectical storytelling. The eight long and short essays are divided into three sub-themes, each of which has essays that provide counterpoints to each other. The first, Witnessing + Memory, highlights the ideas of artist as a witness (Frank Möller) along with an essay on the artist as purveyors of memory and its re-exploration (Sorcha Carey). The second theme, Participation + Hierarchy, explores notion of power in cultural performance both the top-down world of cultural stratification (Nada Švob-Đokić) and the bottom-up view of culture participation (Christine Adams and Btihaj Ajana). Our sub-theme of Performance + Heritage speaks to the creation and proliferation of the museum as multicultural and transnational actors in the Abbie Chessler and Patricia Goff essays, while Tim Slade recalls the experience of creating his documentary on human destruction of cultural monuments.

With this issue, AIA also begins its formal association with the Institute for International Cultural Relations at the University of Edinburgh where I serve as Director. IICR brings interdisciplinary and methodological rigor to the study of international cultural interactions. IICR is situated in a historical University and a city known for its culture. AIA's association with IICR, the University of Edinburgh and the city of Edinburgh provide an interesting landscape from which to examine international cultural relations and their performances.

Scan here to watch a video of "Memorial to Lost Words"
https://www.youtube.com/watch?v=dsosRXQavyA

References

Berger, Peter L. and Thomas Luckmann. (1966) *The Social construction of Reality: A Treatise in the Sociology of Knowledge*. New York: Anchor Books.

Goffman, Erving. (1959) *The Presentation of Self in Everyday Life*. New York: Anchor Books.

Said, Edward. (1978) *Orientalism*. New York: Vintage Books.

Theme 1:

Witnessing + Memory

Colonial Wars and Aesthetic Reworking: The Artist as Moral Witness

Frank Möller

Frank Möller is a Senior Research Fellow at the Tampere Peace Research Institute, University of Tampere, Finland, and the co-convenor of the European Consortium for Political Research (ECPR) Standing Group on Politics and the Arts. He is the author of Visual Peace: Images, Spectatorship, and the Politics of Violence *(2013) and the co-editor of* Art as a Political Witness *(forthcoming). His most recent publication is* Politics and Art, Oxford Handbook Online Political Science *(Oxford University Press).*

Abstract

In this article, I analyze Manuel Botelho's post-factum work on the Portuguese colonial wars and ask whether the artist qualifies as a witness, a political witness or even a moral witness as defined by Avishai Margalit. First, I sketch the historico-political context of the colonial wars and their commemoration in monuments in Portugal. Secondly, I discuss Botelho's aesthetic engagement with soldiers' subject positions during the wars. Thirdly, I review Margalit's approach to being a moral witness. Finally, I think about both Botelho's work in light of Margalit's approach to being a witness and Margalit's approach to being a witness in light of Botelho's work. I argue that Botelho, without being himself a moral witness as defined by Margalit, is an intermediary between the moral witness and the moral community, present and future, helping the members of this community to move from what it *is* like to what it *feels* like to live in extraordinary conditions. Extending the understanding of being a witness by decoupling it from co-presence and contemporaneity will enlarge knowledge and help better understand what it means to witness such highly complex and ambivalent forms of social interaction as independence wars.

Introduction: "During the war, I suffered most from things I didn't witness"

In the quotation that opens this article(Couto 2008:102), not being a witness does not imply the lack of awareness of what happened. Indeed, the protagonist continues by exclaiming: "The atrocities that happened!" What atrocities exactly the protagonist is referring to remains slightly opaque—atrocities committed either during the independence war or the following civil war in Mozambique. Although not having been a witness, she suffered. Being a witness here refers to a conventional understanding in terms of *eye*-witnessing. A witness is a spectator, someone "who is or was present and is able to testify from personal observation."[1] A typical example of such an understanding of being a witness is the following line: "In 1949, the African American scholar and activist W.E.B. Du Bois traveled to Poland, where he witnessed firsthand the rubble left behind by the Nazi occupation and war" (Rothberg 2009:111). In order to be a witness, you have to be on location, witnessing—seeing with your own eyes—that to which you can subsequently testify from own observation.

Recent writings in the social sciences and humanities, however, have expanded the concept of being a witness by critically engaging with four elements: co-presence, contemporaneity, materiality, and eventness (Lindroos and Möller, forthcoming). Being on location when something happened to which one could testify based on own experience is not seen as a precondition for being a witness any more. Furthermore, contemporaneity is no longer required. It is possible to be a witness of something that happened a long time ago. Thus, spatial and temporal distances do not mean that a person cannot be a witness. The third element in the current further development of the concept of being a witness is the identification of material objects, for example photographs, as witnesses. Being a witness has also been de-connected from tragic events and given an everyday dimension, a dimension, however, that I will largely ignore in what follows.

In Mia Couto's story, the protagonist suffers from the atrocities that her husband, "behaving just as the enemy he called devils," committed on the battlefield, atrocities communicated to her in the form of rumors only. At that time, the reports of massacres seemed to "ha[ve] taken place in another

[1] The Shorter Oxford English Dictionary on Historical Principles, Vol. II, prepared by William Little, H.W. Fowler and Jessie Coulson. Revised and edited by C.T. Onions. Third edition, completely reset with etymologies revised by G.W.S. Friedrichsen and with revised addenda. Oxford: Clarendon Press, 1973, p. 2562.

world" (Couto 2008:102). "War," however, "leaves wounds that no amount of time can heal" (Couto 2008:125) — wounds from which not only those against whom atrocities were committed continue to suffer but also those distant witnesses for whom these atrocities were only rumors.

This article is an engagement with the idea of the artist as a witness. It is located in the independence wars fought by then Portuguese colonies in Africa, and it discusses artworks that were produced a long time after these wars ended. But, in a sense, these wars did not end — "war leaves wounds that no amount of time can heal." This open-endedness — "the event-as-aftermath" (Roberts 2014:107) — is one way of understanding the post-factum artist as a witness.[2] The article discusses artworks that were produced by a Portuguese artist, Manuel Botelho, an artist who did not participate in these wars; nevertheless, he suffered from them or, more precisely, from his nonparticipation in wars in which he was supposed to participate. Artists like Botelho may be witnesses of atrocities they were supposed to commit but didn't, of suffering they were supposed to inflict on others and endure themselves but didn't, and of experiences they were supposed to make but didn't.

I refer to this artist as a witness, and it is one purpose of this article to try to understand what kind of witness he is. All the things he did *not* do render difficult a conventional understanding of him as a witness. Another purpose of this article is to get engaged with the dichotomy victim–perpetrator aiming, without belittling the suffering of the victims, to show its inadequacy in this particular historical case. I do not make any claims beyond the case I investigate in this article. The third, and final, purpose of this article is the investigation of the idea of the artist as a *moral* witness, derived from Avishai Margalit's work. While this seems to be an ambitious objective for an article, I would argue that these three objectives are inter-connected and that engagement with all of them in one article is not only possible but, indeed, necessary.

The first step is to sketch the historico-political context of the colonial wars and their commemoration in monuments in Portugal. In a second step, I present and discuss Botelho's aesthetic engagement with soldiers' subject positions during the wars. In a third step, I review Margalit's concept of being a moral witness. Finally, staging a kind of imagined dialog between a scholar and an artist, I think about both Botelho's work in light of Margalit's approach to being a witness and Margalit's approach to being a witness in light of

[2] For "the post-factum witness," see Lowe (2014:228).

Botelho's work. By doing so, I hope not only to be able to understand what kind of witness Botelho is but also to engage critically with such categories as risk, co-presence, and contemporaneity, all of which are central to our understanding of what it means to be a witness. I present first the works of art and the historical context without which they would not exist and then the theoretical framework within which I discuss these works of art. I have chosen this order to respect the interpretative openness that every work of art carries with it and to invite readers to engage with Botelho's art on their own terms. Beginning this article by establishing a theoretical framework would almost inevitably have predetermined readers' engagement with the following artworks and thus infringed upon the variety of meanings readers may assign to them.[3]

"To what deaths, what miseries you condemn / Your heroes! What pains you inflict on them ..." (Camões 2001:96)

From 1961[4] to 1974, the Portuguese authorities fought wars in what they, in accordance with the Portuguese constitution of the time, referred to as *provincias ultramarinas* or Ultramar, overseas territories or provinces (Afonso and Gomes 2010; Cann 2012; Venter 2015). The purpose of these wars, following the logic of sovereignty, territorial integrity, and portuguesismo (Portugueseness), was to prevent these territories from becoming independent states. The "overseas territories" were indeed seen as integral parts of Portugal rather than as colonies and the Colonial Act of 1930 was replaced by terminology revolving around the idea of Ultramar. This understanding was expressed in slogans such as *De Minho a Timor somos todos portugueses* (from the Minho to Timor we are all Portuguese) and in concepts like *unidade da nação pluricontinental portugues* (Portugal as multicontinental nation) (see Figure 1).[5]

---

[3] I would like to thank the reviewer for Arts and International Affairs for their constructive engagement with an earlier draft of this article and especially for encouragement to go beyond merely "applying" Margalit's concept to Botelho's work. I would also like to thank Manuel Botelho for permission to reproduce his works of art in this article and Carole Garton for wonderful translations from the Portuguese.

[4] As Piçarra (2014:92–93) explains, the first organized uprising against Portuguese rule in Africa, an attack on a prison in the neighborhood of Sambizanga, Luanda, took place in 1961 and is referenced in Sarah Maldoror's film Sambizanga (1972).

[5] Figures 1–9: author's photographs; Figures 10–13: artworks by Manuel Botelho, reproduced by permission; Figures 14 and 15: artworks and photographs by Manuel Botelho, used by permission.

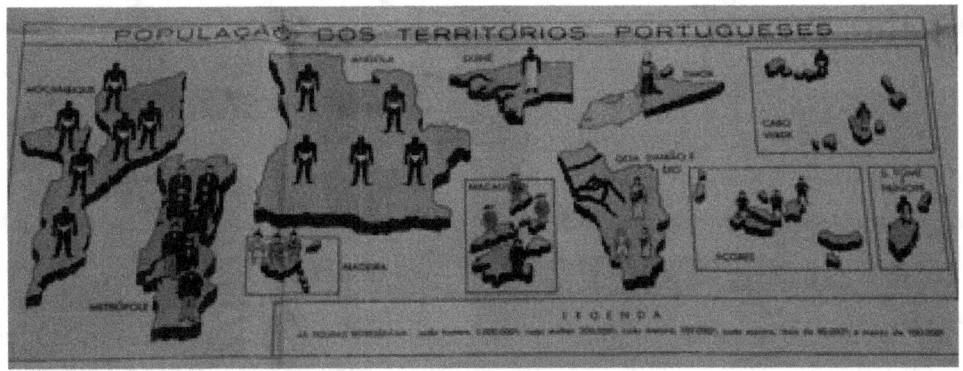

Figure 1. Portugal adjacente e ultramarine (mapa escolar) by João Maria Carlos Moreira da Silva (detail); photograph taken at the occasion of the exhibition *RETORNAR: Traços de Memória*, Galeria Av. da Índia, Lisbon, February 2, 2016

Based on this understanding, the 1955 Bandung conference condemning "colonialism in all its manifestations" and the United Nations Declaration on the Granting of Independence to Colonial Countries and Peoples of December 14, 1960 (resolution 1514) were considered irrelevant for Portugal. With the revolution of April 25, 1974, the wars were, from the official Portuguese perspective, lost. Mozambique, Angola, Guinea-Bissau, Cape Verde and São Tomé e Príncipe were internationally recognized as independent states. Portugal established what Graham (2009:75), before the current economic crisis and its political ramifications, calls a "noisy, messy, healthy democracy." The memory of the overseas wars is institutionalized in Portugal across the country in various monuments featuring strikingly different approaches to design and architecture (see Figures 2 and 3). These monuments are maintained by the Combatants League (Liga dos combatentes) which was established after the Great War as the Great War Combatants League to support the soldiers and their families. The name was changed into Combatants League on December 16, 1975 so that the organization could extend its activities to include soldiers from what the League still refers to as Overseas Wars, despite the term's profound de-legitimation due to its association with the dictatorship.

The purpose of these memorials is to honor the soldiers who died in the service of Portugal (Figure 4), those who died while defending the overseas territories (Figure 5), and those who died in the overseas campaigns (Figure 6).

The purpose of these memorials is to acknowledge the suffering that the Portuguese soldiers endured during the wars; especially those who died are remembered and honored. Their death may be regrettable. However, linked to a noble cause—"serviço de Portugal," for example—death is at least acceptable. Anonymous death, however, is not acceptable. *Anonymous* death, however, is not acceptable.[6] The central monument in Belém, inaugurated on January 15, 1994, is impressive by dint of its architecture (Figure 3) but primarily owing to the huge number of what Simpson (2006:41), in a different context, calls "names cut in stone" (Figure 7). As I explain elsewhere (2013:141), these names are "arrayed—disciplined—in columns, their military ranks added, resembling and reproducing military forms of organization and arrangements in line, pretending order, denying the chaos of war." The dead "can offer no resistance to being referred to as 'combatants,' although they or some of them might have wished to be remembered in subject positions other than that of combatants."

Occasionally, the range of people remembered seems wider. Some monuments are dedicated to both the Great War and the Overseas Wars. The Monumento aos combatentes do ultramar in Belém also honors those soldiers who died in peace and humanitarian operations. As the name indicates, however, the monument's main focus is on the colonial wars. The alleged aim of this monument is to contribute to "the unification of all the peoples involved in the Overseas Wars" and this may seem to invite people other than Portuguese soldiers to contribute to this unification. A closer reading of design and inscriptions, however, shows that this is not the case (Möller 2013:132–151).

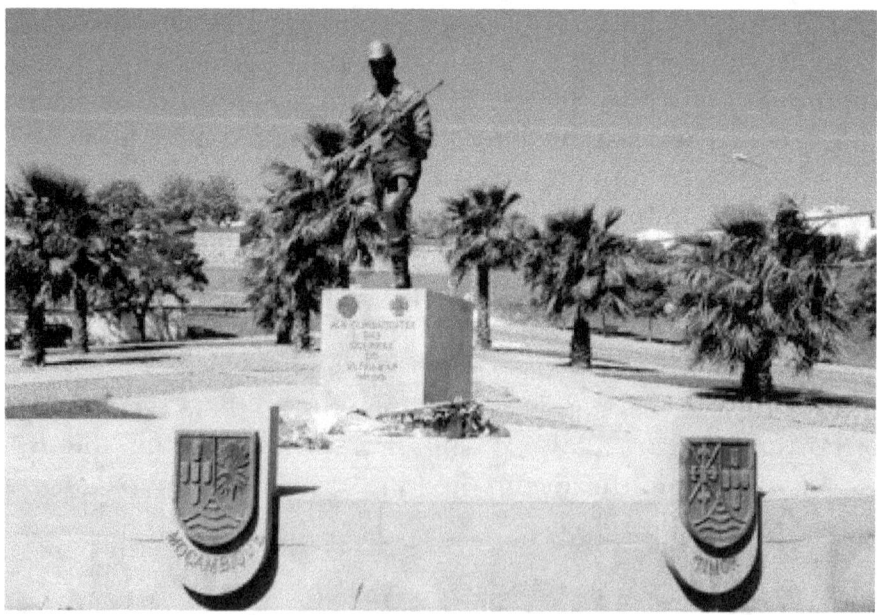

Figure 2. Monumento aos combatentes das guerras do ultramar, Elvas

[6] One ingredient of the Memorial ao Combatente, inaugurated November 11, 2015, is the reading of the names of the Portuguese soldiers who died in the context of the Great War.

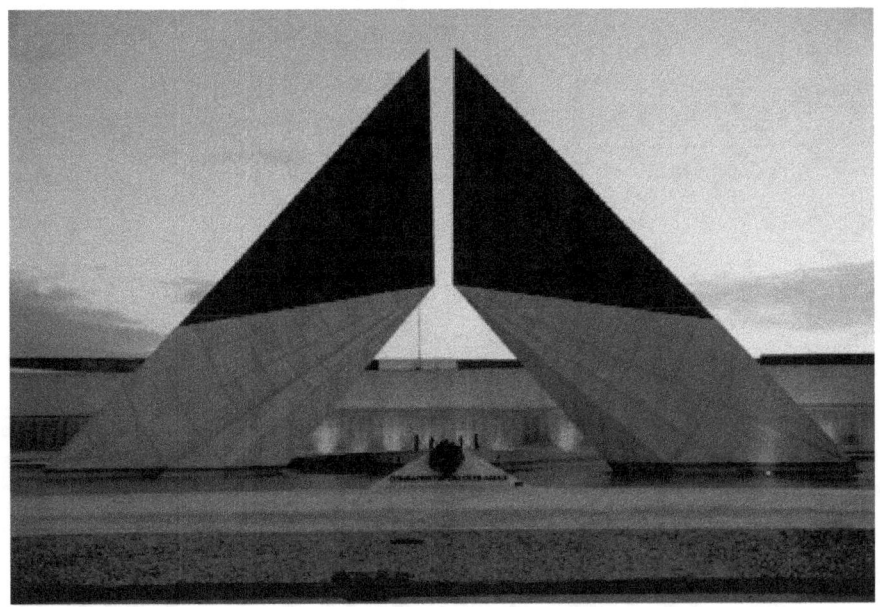

Figure 3. Monumento aos combatentes do ultramar, Belém

"… poor cornered animals filled with evil and terror" (Antunes 2008:205)

The colonial wars are remembered not only in monuments but also in art including visual art. Photography, for example, has had a long and complex relationship with colonialism. This relationship is explored in a recent publication analyzing such issues as anthropological modes of classifying and registering colonial subjects, olonial subjects, othe production of knowledge by means of photographs, and the circulation, dissemination, and reproduction patterns of colonial photographs (Vicente 2014). The timeframe of this publication largely excludes the colonial wars (see, however, Laranjeiro 2014). The atrocities committed by European colonial powers on African subjects and photographically documented are well known and critically discussed in international studies (see Patrick 2014). The context of Portuguese colonialism, however, is under explored (see, however, Ramos 2014). Portuguese colonialism collapsed before soldier photography emerged as a widely disseminated mass phenomenon (Struck 2011). Thus, the visual material available is limited.[7] It was also an era of censorship by the

[7] However, in recent years, several autobiographies on the colonial wars have been published, many of which include photographs. The analysis of these writings and photographs is beyond the scope of this article just as is the evaluation of the material, visual and otherwise, collected in the Arquivo Histórico Ultramar in Lisbon.

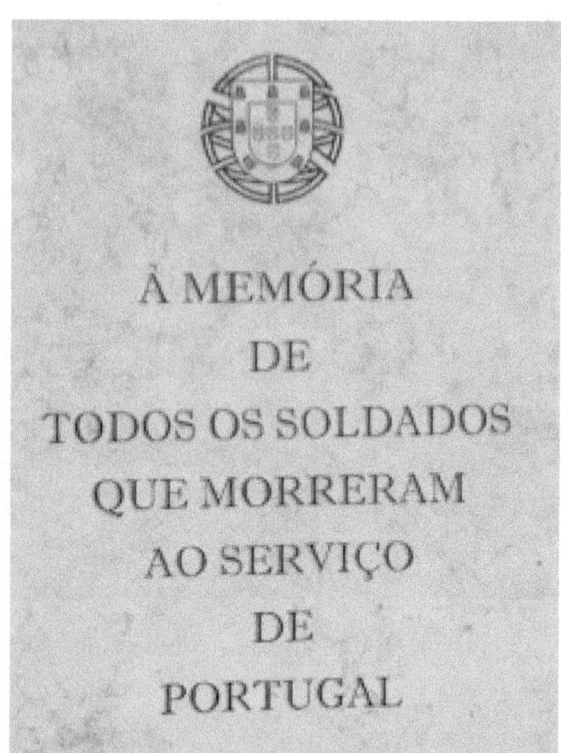

À MEMÓRIA
DE
TODOS OS SOLDADOS
QUE MORRERAM
AO SERVIÇO
DE
PORTUGAL

Figure 4. Monumento aos combatentes do ultramar, Belém

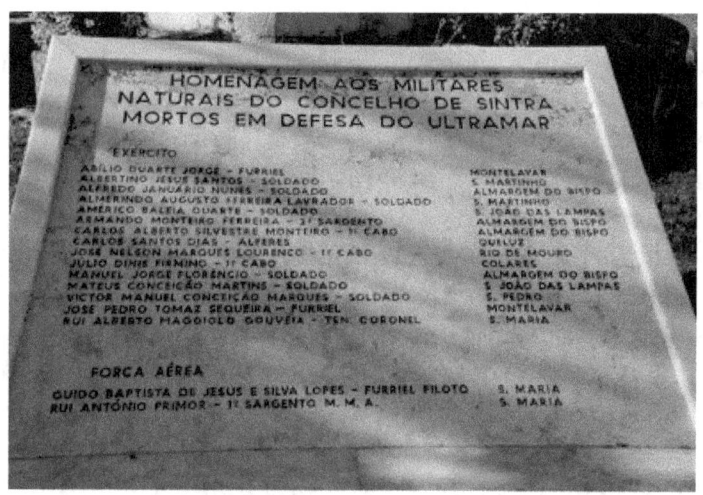

Figure 5. Homenagem aos militares naturais do concelho de Sintra mortos em defesa do ultramar, Sintra

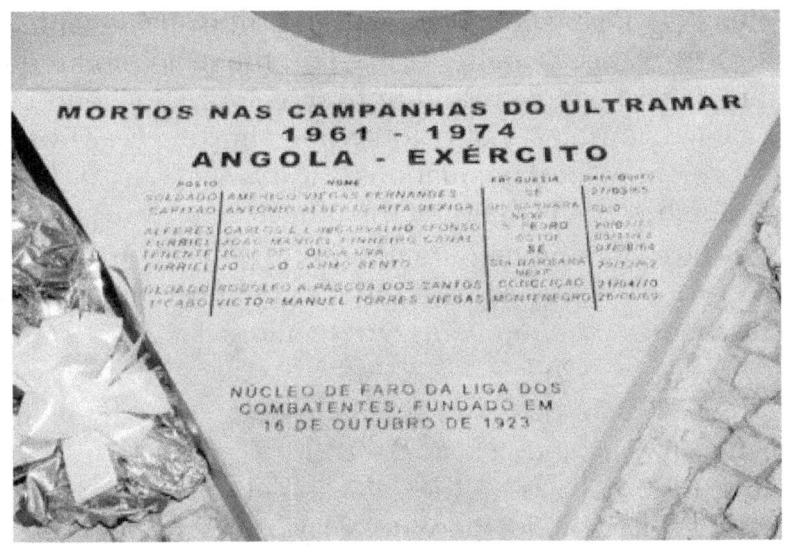

Figure 6. Mortos nas campanhas do ultramar 1961–1974, Faro

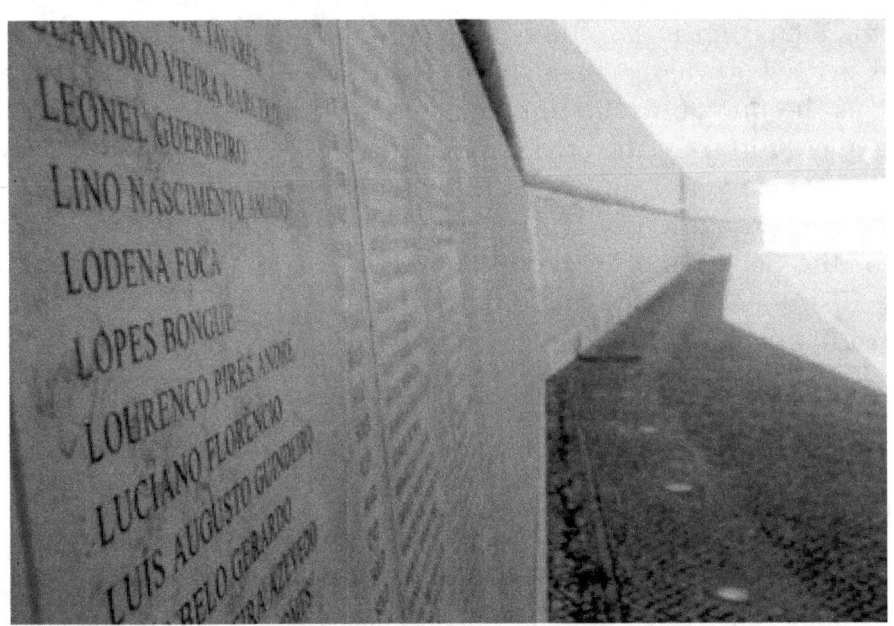

Figure 7. Monumento aos combatentes do ultramar, Belém

Portuguese authorities, the *Estado Novo*. The analysis of the state's attempts to shape the image of Portuguese colonialism in films has established that those films that escaped censorship focused on the idealization of colonial life, depicted modernization as resulting from colonization, and cultivated *portuguesismo* while ignoring social realities and showing very little interest in the living conditions of local populations (Piçarra 2014). Just as filmmakers, during the dictatorship, tried to correct the official view by means of diverse cinematographic strategies aiming to circumvent censorship (Piçarra 2014), artists nowadays critically engage with representations of the colonial wars and their remembrance in monuments and memorials.

Portuguese artists do not necessarily incorporate into their work the suffering inflicted by Portuguese soldiers on local populations. They share with the monuments emphasis on the suffering of the Portuguese soldiers. Their approaches to victimhood, therefore, may be criticized as Eurocentric. However, they are different from the approaches underlying the monuments. First, works of art lack the pathos and solemn language characteristic of the monuments. Artists are not searching for the meaning of the deaths of the soldiers; on the contrary, they visualize precisely the lack of meaning, the senselessness, and absurdity of these deaths and suffering. Secondly, monuments focus on those soldiers who died during wars (Winter 1995:78). Works of art acknowledge that survival does not mean the absence of suffering, as the quotation that opened this part indicates just as does the following quotation from the same book (Antunes 2008:241): "months upon months of perplexity and suffering. […] maybe so many months of war had transformed us into indecisive, useless creatures, into pitiful drunkards waiting for the paleness of dawn, to later wait for afternoon and night in the same disinterested surrender." Elsewhere, Antunes (2012:141) has his protagonist hallucinate as follows:

> We weren't mad dogs when we arrived here, I said to the lieutenant, who was seething with anger and indignation, we weren't mad dogs before the censored letters, the attacks, the ambushes, the mines, the lack of food and tobacco and cold drinks and matches and water and coffins, before we were told that a Berliet truck was worth more than a man and before we found out that the death of a soldier merited just three lines in the newspaper.

Those who stayed at home—families, friends, and loved ones—also suffered despite the lack of personal and physical involvement in the wars. They suffered from being aware of the dangers the soldiers were exposed to and, as the discussion that opened this article shows, also from the awareness of the atrocities the soldiers, or at least some of them, were likely to commit during the war. And the young soldiers, "drafted originally for two years, but often serving for up to four" (Chabal 2002:14), were "disillusioned" (Chabal 2002:14) and unprepared for guerilla warfare. Having been dispatched as conscripts by an authoritarian regime, they could not normally themselves decide whether they wished to participate in the wars or not: the option not to participate in a seemingly unwinnable and hopeless war existed for only a minority of young people. Dictator Salazar's "own personnel commitment" to the Portuguese presence in Africa and "his propensity to brook no opposition" dominated "any voice of reason" and made "retreat or compromise over African affairs" impossible (Cann 2012:47). Opposition was translated into an ever more intransigent position on Portugal's presence *ultramar* up to the 1974 revolution, backed by a powerful secret police operating both in Portugal and in the colonies.[8]

Thus, without ignoring or minimizing the suffering inflicted on local populations *by* Portuguese soldiers and without denying the power discrepancies between colonizers and colonized, the suffering inflicted *on* Portuguese soldiers and their relatives by their political and military leadership should not be ignored. After all, the soldiers soon realized that "the generals in air-conditioned Luanda invented a war in which we would die and they would live" (Antunes 2012:150). They understood that one objective of the war, waged "in the name of a lot of cynical ideas no one believe[d] in," was "to defend the wealth of the three or four families who shore up the regime" (Antunes 2012:141). I am fully aware of the dangers inherent in discussing what might be seen as the victimization of the perpetrators. I am certainly not arguing that the "real" victims of colonialism are the soldiers sent from Europe to defend the colonial project.[9] That would be absurd, even obscene. Addressing the suffering of the Portuguese soldiers does not imply the denial of the suffering they inflicted on others or an attempt at "ranking" suffering. Rather, it offers the possibility to see *both* the suffering inflicted on them by a dictatorial political regime *and* the suffering they inflicted on others; it thus addresses a double dimension of suffering and enables a more differentiated understanding of suffering than does the crude binary perpetrator–victim that, as every binary, hides as much as

[8] In 1974, 65% of the political police force worked in the colonies. Overall, the political police force had 3530 agents (Aljube — a voz das vítimas; see note 22).

[9] See Rothberg (2009:66–107) for "Eurocentric pitfalls" (p. 87) in selected anticolonial discourses.

[10] In his psychoanalytic approach to perpetrator trauma, LaCapra (1998:41) argues that such trauma, "while attended by symptoms that may be comparable to those of victims, is ethically and politically different in decisive ways" from victim trauma. I acknowledge these differences.

it reveals.[10] It not only renders possible analysis of the inter-relationship between these two dimensions, but also complicates our understanding of victims and perpetrators; perpetrators can, to some extent, be victims, too, "transformed … into people we weren't before, that we'd never been, into poor cornered animals filled with evil and terror. In the depths of our yellow eyes wailed a panicked childhood fear, a mute timid panic clouded by hesitation and shame" (Antunes 2008:205). The reduction to two opposing subject positions—victim versus perpetrator—in such dynamic, ambivalent, chaotic, and complex social interactions as independence wars offers only limited satisfaction. As noted in many contexts, a strict dichotomy perpetrator versus victim is analytically insufficient. Rothberg (2009:95), for example, notes "the permeable relation, in cultural texts as well as in history, between enemies 'inside' and 'outside' of empire as well as between 'perpetrators' and 'victims' and 'enemies' and 'friends.'"[11] Fujii, in her micro-study on the 1994 genocide in Rwanda, shows how pre-conceived notions of "survivor" and "perpetrator" can collapse when scrutinized thoroughly in light of empirical evidence (2009:36–37). It is in this context that art can assume an eminently political character—not by taking sides and simplifying but by complicating and showing the complexities of human interactions. Indeed, Camões (2001:96), writing in 1572, was aware of these complexities when he included in *Os Lusíadas* (*The Lusíads*)—the famous epic critically celebrating the Portuguese overseas expansion—the voice of the Old Man of Belém who warned against the fallacies underlying the politics of expansion:

O pride of power! O futile lust
For that vanity known as fame!
That hollow conceit which puffs itself up
And which popular cant calls honour!
What punishment, what poetic justice,
You exact on souls that pursue you!
To what deaths, what miseries you condemn
Your heroes! What pains you inflict on them!

You wreck all peace of soul and body,
You promote separation and adultery;
Subtly, manifestly, you consume
The wealth of kingdoms and empires!
They call distinction, they call honour
What deserves ridicule and contempt;
They talk of glory and eternal fame,
And men are driven frantic by a name!

[11] See also Agamben (2002:20–21) and Levi (1989:36–69).p. 87) in selected anticolonial discourses.

And his fellow writer, Pessoa (1996:292), writing in 1916, had his alter ego, Bernardo Soares, declare: "No empire justifies breaking a child's doll. No ideal is worth the sacrifice of a toy train." Such insights provided by poets were ignored by the state authorities.[12] However, this ignorance has not deterred artists from continuing to engage critically with the colonial wars.

Matchbox, Christmas messages, aerograms and diaries—Manuel Botelho's work

One of the artists who has dedicated a huge portion of his work to the memory of the colonial wars and the suffering of the soldiers during these wars is, paradoxically it seems, a person who had, and used, the option *not* to participate in the wars. Born in 1950, Manuel Botelho belongs to the very generation that experienced the colonial wars directly and personally. Botelho, however, was not one of the "men of [his] generation" who, in the artist's words, "set sail such a long time ago for Angola, Guinea and Mozambique, hidden behind a camouflaged uniform and a G3" and with whom he increasingly wishes "to be identified." At the time of the 1974 revolution, Botelho was a last-year student of architecture and thus "didn't have to endure the experience of being involved in a live war. But I lived through it intensely, in a state of obsessive anticipation that lasted throughout my youth." Botelho, while "march[ing] through the streets shouting 'no more soldiers to the colonies,' began to have guilt feelings about not having shared in this period of abnegation and self-sacrifice" (quoted in Porfírio 2010:73–74). He translated these guilt feelings into the role of "an artist–witness," gathering "objects and images, memories and fears, both his own and those of others" (Porfírio 2010:72).

In one installation, maps project the outlines of Portugal's colonial territories on a European map. The installation titled *Matchbox: Portugal* is not a small country (2009) can be read as an ironic engagement with the empty pomposity and shallow grandiosity of the official rhetoric in terms of *portuguesismo*—the attempt, by all possible means, to stick to the myth of multicontinental Portugal so as to "to preserve the Salazar regime" (Cann 2012:45) which found itself internationally increasingly isolated, and to avoid Portugal's reduction to a small, and ultimately politically irrelevant, European state. At the same time, the map projection shows the absurd discrepancy as regards size and territory and, with it, the futility of the colonial wars, bound to failure.[13]

[12] On the power of poetry in the context of international relations, see Bleiker (2009).
[13] See the artist's website http://manuelbotelho.com/pt/index.php?/work/2009--mensagens-de-natal--matchbox (accessed July 28, 2016).

Another installation titled *Inventário: Mensagens de Natal* (2008) features a number of television screens endlessly repeating original footage of Christmas messages the soldiers had for those at home. These messages were transmitted by Rádio e Televisão de Portugal (RTP) from the theaters of war, intended to document the soldiers' wellbeing. In the installation's loop, however, the standardized texts the soldiers were permitted to utter prove exactly the opposite (Figures 8 and 9).

Aerogramas para 2010 (Figures 10–13) engages with a free transport system for messages from the colonies, offered by Transportes Aéreos Portugueses (TAP). Anticipating terminology to be introduced in the next section, it can be said that this transport system served as a link between those who had knowledge-by-acquaintance of suffering and those who had not; between those who personally experienced actual suffering and those who did not; and between those who took risks and those who did not. This system is alluded to in a fusion of drawings and handwritten texts reproducing letters or instructions for use from the original aerograms (Porfírio 2010:73). The texts include statements by nowadays rather well-known figures such as Antunes whom I quoted above. More important than the current celebrity status of some of the letters' authors are two things. First, as Rothberg (2009:203) notes in his discussion of Charlotte Delbo's *Les belles lettres*, "memory in the form of letters (understood broadly) can take part in the necessary task of re-forming what counts as public and, therefore, what is politically thinkable." Secondly, the letters were written by people who, in contrast to the artist, were on location when something happened to which they could—and did—testify based on own experience; they were eye-witnesses of both the suffering they inflicted on others and the suffering inflicted on them. These texts increase both the authenticity of the artworks and their emotional and affective power. They strengthen what I would like to call the artworks' having-been-there-ness.

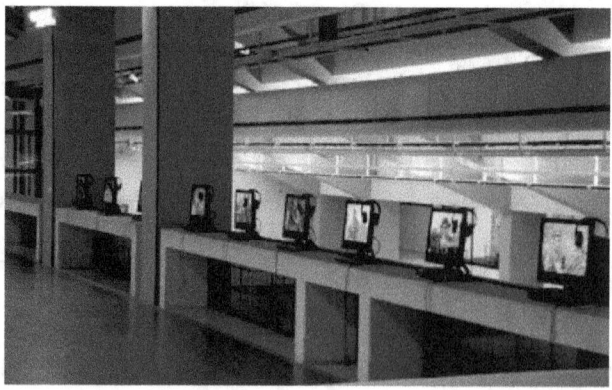

Figure 8. Manuel Botelho, Inventário: Mensagens de Natal (2008); photograph taken at the occasion of the exhibition Professores, Centro de Arte Moderna, Fundação Calouste Gulbenkian, Lisbon, December 2, 2010

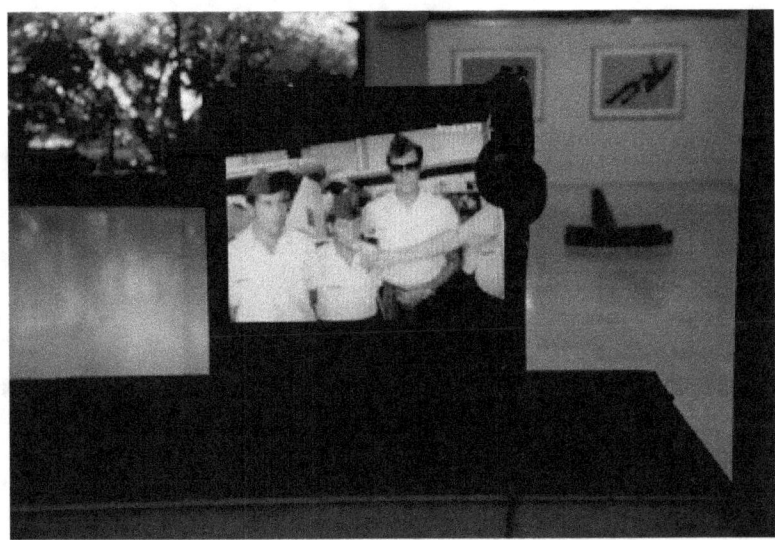

Figure 9. Manuel Botelho, *Inventário: Mensagens de Natal* (2008); photograph taken at the occasion of the exhibition *Professores*, Centro de Arte Moderna, Fundação Calouste Gulbenkian, Lisbon, December 2, 2010 (detail).

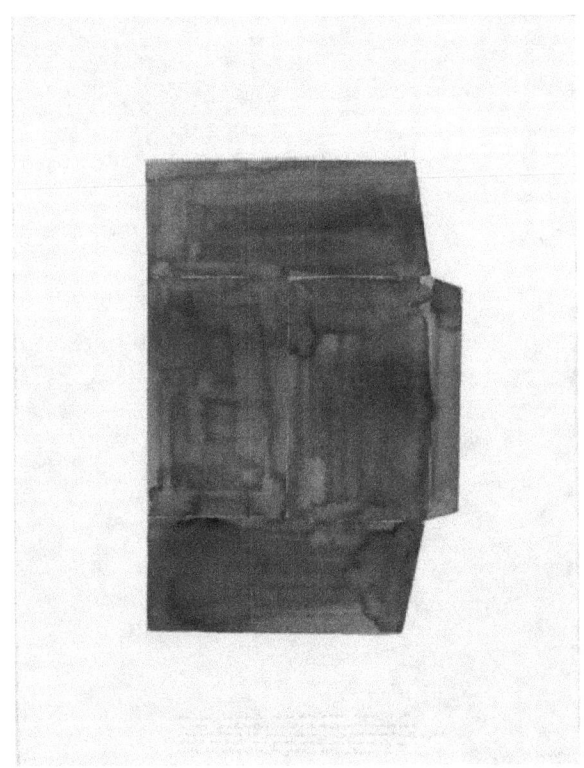

Figure 10. Manuel Botelho, *Desculpa as cartas brutais que por vezes te mando* (inclui excerto de aerograma de Mário Beja Santos) (*Forgive the brutal letters I often sent you; with a quote from an aerogram* by Mário Beja Santos), 2009, pencil and watercolor on paper, 66 x 50.5 cm2. (Courtesy: The artist)

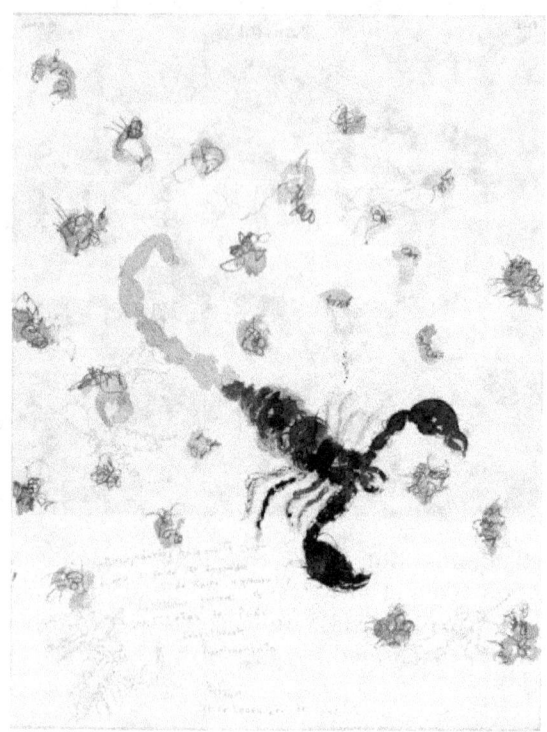

Figure 11. Manuel Botelho, *Despedida* (inclui excerto de depoimento de Mário Graça Abreu) (*Farewell*, with a quote from a statement by Mário Graça Abreu), 2009, pencil and watercolor on paper, 66 x 50.5 cm2. (Courtesy: The artist)

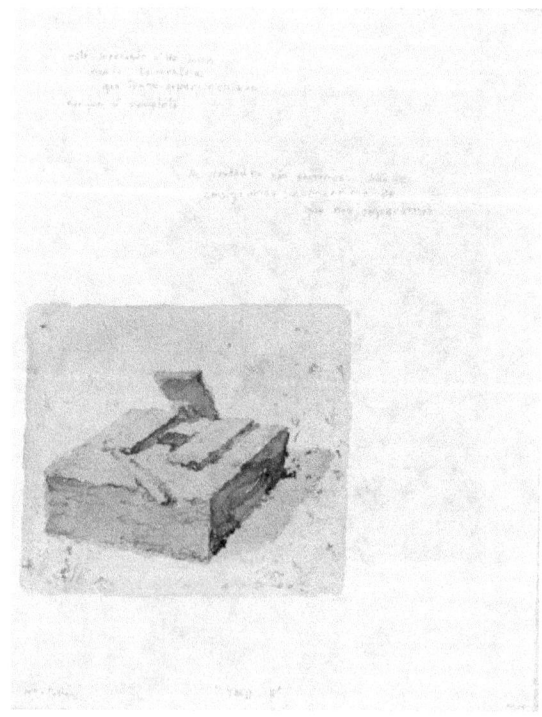

Figure 12. Manuel Botelho, *TMD-8*, 2009, pencil and watercolor on paper, 66 x 50.5 cm2. (Courtesy: The artist)

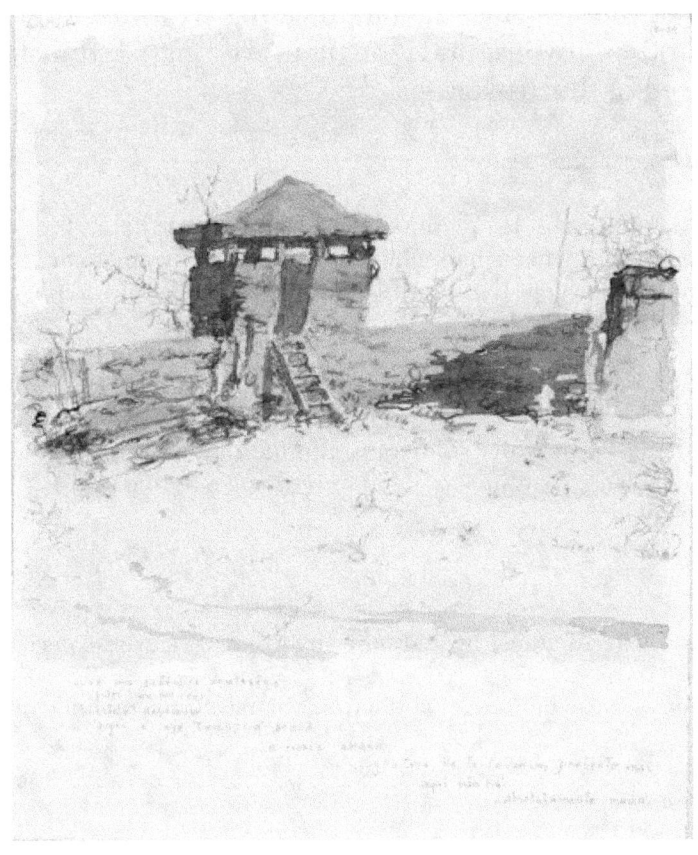

Figure 13. Manuel Botelho, *Aqui não há absolutamente nada* (inclui excerto de aerograma de Manuel Beça Múrias) (*There is absolutely nothing here*; with a quote from an aerogram by Manuel Beça Múrias (2009)), pencil and watercolor on paper, 66 x 50.5 cm2. (Courtesy: The artist)

As Bleiker (2009:4) explains, even in a world dominated by images "we ultimately need words to make sense of our world. Language ... is the process through which we represent and make sense of ourselves and our surroundings: the cultural crystallization of who we are as people." Words, incorporated into drawings, speak to us together with the drawings. This "speaking together" may capitalize on what Gilgen (2003:56) calls a mutually supportive "intellectual stereoscopic effect: the image gains in profile through the verbal information conveyed in the caption; from the accompanying image this information gains persuasive power." The texts are important because they link the works of art with what happened "such a long time ago [in] Angola, Guinea and Mozambique" (Botelho) to which the artist cannot himself testify from own experience. They are important as

29

integral parts of the drawings communicating with the drawings and also as testimony in their own right. Here, then, are English translations[14] of the texts reproduced in the artworks:

Forgive the brutal letters I often sent you

sorry about the violent letters I sometimes send you. I admit that at times I feel very hurt that you don't understand what is happening here but then I come to my senses and realize that it is very difficult to accept that there's another war going on when it isn't included in newspapers or on the radio and TV.

Farewell

Yesterday, Saturday, a lot of white soldiers were bidding farewell to Guinea, in search of their final pleasures. The prostitutes of Pilão were doing a heroic job.
Bissau December 16, 1973.

TMD-8

this separation is one of the most heart-rendering things I've ever experienced. Because it is total.
My longing for you is overwhelming. I still haven't managed to convince myself that we are separated …

There is absolutely nothing here

… this is utter desolation,
  believe me,
   it's desolating …
  what we have here is sand …
        and more sand
          … I'd like to get you a present but
            here there isn't
              absolutely anything

Recent writings in the social sciences and humanities have decoupled the concept of being a witness from personal observation. In its most radical reformulation, the concept of being a witness does not refer to *people* anymore but to *material objects*. Photographs, for example, appear as witnesses in Azoulay's work (2014:129) and as "social agents … bearing witness to past events" in Lowe's work (2014:213). It is in this context that another Botelho installation, appropriately titled *Contagem Descrescente 1967–1969 (Countdown)*, is important: soldier diaries, but particular diaries largely devoid of text (Figures 14 and 15). These diaries are, as Porfírio (2010:73) explains,

[14] Translated from the Portuguese by Carole Garton; translations used by permission.

"immediately recognizable by anyone who directly experienced that prison which was also the war."They consist of nothing else than numbers indicating the amount of days a soldier had still to serve, and survive, until the end of the commission (o final da comissão). Collected from flea markets, these documents communicate pain, terror and boredom ("there is absolutely nothing here"; see Figure 13); they symbolize the seeming endlessness of each and every day that had to pass before yet another number could be crossed. The artist's approach is minimalistic. No additional language is required, just numbers from 1 to 732 or lists of years, months, and weeks. Despite their materiality, these documents cannot be limited to materiality; they are "inextricably connected with individual people." At the same time, they show "the shared experience of a generation"—the men of Botelho's generation (Möller 2013:156). Are these diaries witnesses, perhaps even moral witnesses?

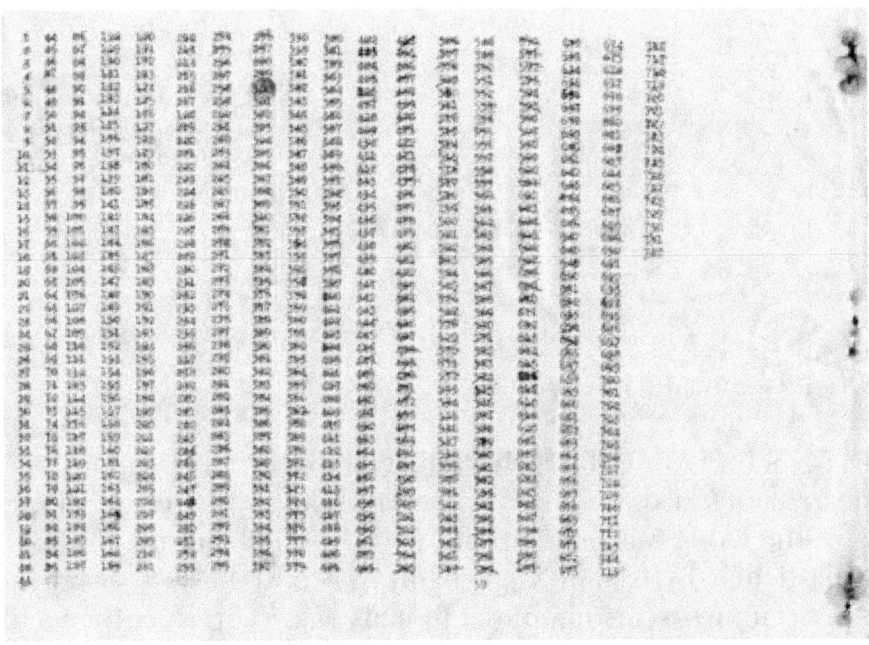

Figure 14. Manuel Botelho, *Contagem Descrescente 1967–1969* (1). Photograph: Manuel Botelho. (Courtesy: The artist)

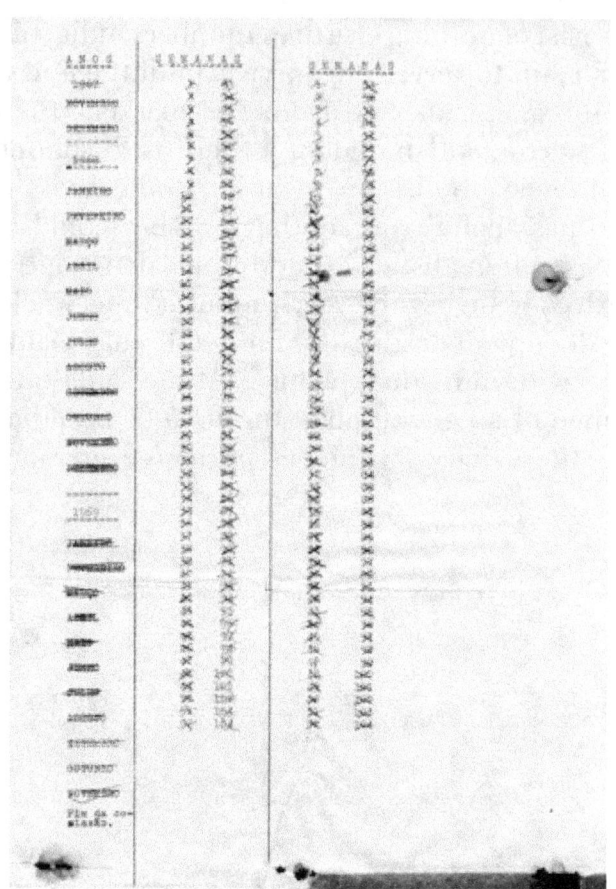

Figure 15. Manuel Botelho, *Contagem Descrescente 1967–1969* (2). Photograph: Manuel Botelho. (Courtesy: The artist)

The (artist as) moral witness

Wieviorka (2006), writing about Holocaust memories and the politics of these memories, characterizes the 1970s and early 1980s as the "era of the witness." The era of the witness is one conditioned by visual culture. Audiovisuality, used in particular by Claude Lanzmann, not only helped systematize the collection of survivors' testimonies, but it also gave survivors the feeling that someone was listening—and watching. An audience listening to survivors' testimonies is what survivors need, and this audience was largely absent prior to the era of the witness. Wieviorka does not address the question of whether or not such artists as Lanzmann can be witnesses of events they did not personally experience but she notes that survivors' testimonies can be transformed into artworks. She does not ask whether or not this is what survivors want. However, this transformation does not seem to have undermined the evidentiary qualities of the testimonies. These testimonies are not watched and listened to because of the aesthetic quality of the film that presents them or because of the ingenuity—including occasional ruthlessness—of the film's director or because of the way the film thinks.[15] It is ultimately the testimonies that matter, not their transformation into film, although the director's cinematographic approach, problematic as it may be, may help spectators to think about what they saw and listened to. It may help spectators to *believe* the witnesses despite the seeming incredibility—in the sense of *beyond belief*—of the testimonies.[16] This is what survivors need, too. Wieviorka (2006:xiv) concludes that discourses and practices revolving around the Holocaust and the memory of the Holocaust have "become, for better or for worse, the definitive model for memory construction." The use of audiovisuality helped establish these discourses and practices as models (and this assessment does by no means call into question the power of such testimonies as Primo Levi's books that do not rely on audiovisual culture).[17]

Rothberg has demonstrated that the era of the witness would hardly have come into existence in the way it did without the preceding and parallel era of decolonization and the discourses both revolving around it and making it possible. Rothberg emphasizes cross-fertilization, interrelationships, and interactions among different discourses. Rothberg (2009:113) stresses "the need for a comparative approach to the multidirectionality of collective memory that considers questions of politics, aesthetics, and the public sphere in a nonreductive, transnational framework." In light of Rothberg's argumentation, it makes sense to analytically decouple concepts that have been developed in connection with the Holocaust from the Holocaust (without denying the uniqueness of the Holocaust or relativizing it) and to think about the question of what these writings—altered, further developed, specified in light of specific cases—tell us about other cases and other memory constructions as well (just as it makes sense to proceed the other way round and ask what other memory discourses reveal about the construction of Holocaust memory). Margalit's (2004) concept of the *moral witness*, referenced in international studies in Danchev's work on the artist as moralist (2009:3), is a case in point. What can we learn about the memories of the independence wars in Africa by thinking about them in

---

[15]Shapiro (2009) explores how films think.
[16]Korhonen (2008:115) argues that testimony "relies on an act of faith: we must choose whether we believe the witness or nor."
[17]Rothberg (2009:175–198) connects audio-visual technologies with the emergence of the survivor as a public figure in his discussion of both the Eichmann trial and its televisual broadcast and Jean Rouch and Edgar Morin's film Chronique d'un été (1960–1961), i.e., years before the Lanzmann film.

terms of Margalit's suggestion in the context of the Holocaust? Does such thinking produce new knowledge on these wars? What can we learn about the artist as a witness? What, then, does Margalit write about being a witness and, in particular, how does he understand the moral witness?

In his most rigorous definition, Margalit (2004:149) defines the (paradigmatic) moral witness as a person with "knowledge-by-acquaintance of suffering."[18] Knowledge-by-acquaintance refers to both *personal* experience and *actual* experience of "suffering inflicted by an unmitigated evil regime" (p. 148). Being a moral witness refers to the *experience* of suffering, not just the *observation* of suffering. If this were all Margalit had to say about the moral witness, then I could stop my investigation here. However, an *observer* can be a moral witness on condition that he or she is "at personal risk." This risk can come in two variations: the one defined as "belonging to the category of people toward whom the evil deeds are directed" and the other defined as attempts "to document and record what happens for some future use" (p. 150).[19] The use of the present tense here links Margalit's definition to the conventional understanding of being a witness with its emphasis on contemporaneity discussed earlier just as does his emphasis on the *eye* witness; indeed, "the authority of a moral witness comes from being an eyewitness" (p. 173).[20] Artists documenting or recording the suffering of others for some future use would seem to qualify as moral witnesses but, again, there are two conditions: first, their "testimonial mission has [to have] a moral purpose" (p. 151) and, secondly, they have to take risks. "To be a moral witness … is all about taking risks" (p. 157). The idea that the risk-taking observer documenting what happens "for some future use" qualifies as moral witness thus needs specification: the future use cannot be separated from the testimonial mission's moral purpose. But the very idea of a *future use* is hard to reconcile with Margalit's emphasis on the "intrinsic value" of testimony, its noninstrumentality: testimony is not a means to an end and this is especially true with regard to the paradigmatic moral witness (p. 167). Ultimately, the subject position of moral witness cannot be thought of without "hope: that in another place or another time there exists, or will exist, a moral community that will listen to their testimony" (p. 155).

[18] The following page references in the text are for this book.
[19] As will become clear shortly, the issue here is not for "some future use" but is a very specific one.
[20] Such a strong focus on the eyewitness might be irritating given the notorious unreliability of eyewitness reports observed by, for example, Levi (1989:23). The moral witness, however, is not primarily interested in the factual truth (see below).

Margalit does not only differentiate the *witness* from the *moral* witness and the moral witness from the *paradigmatic* moral witness, but he also differentiates the moral witness from the *political* witness. While the one's testimony has an intrinsic value, the other "believes that the incriminating evidence that she gathers is an instrument in the war effort" (p. 167). This differentiation is puzzling for two reasons. First, an "unmitigated evil regime" can display evil without being engaged in a war effort. Secondly, gathering incriminating evidence as an instrument in a war effort would seem to be in accordance with Margalit's understanding, quoted above, that a moral witness is he or she who documents and records what happens for some future use; gathering evidence as an instrument in a war effort is surely in accordance with the moral purpose of a testimonial mission, which is the precondition for being a moral witness. Another reason for differentiating the moral witness from the political witness lies in the difference between "telling it like it was" and "telling it like it felt." Margalit (p. 168) writes:

> The political witness, by temperament and training, can be a much better witness than the mere moral witness for the structure of evil and not only for episodes of evil. And thus he can be a more valuable witness in uncovering the factual truth. The political witness can be very noble in fighting evil against all odds. And yet as an ideal type, although his features partly overlap with those of the moral witness, the political witness is still distinct, not to be confused with the moral witness. Both are engaged in uncovering what evil tries to cover up. The political witness may be more effective in uncovering the factual truth, in telling it like it was. But the moral witness is more valuable at telling it like it felt, that is, telling what it was like to be subjected to such evil. The first-person accounts of moral witnesses are essential to what they report, whereas political witnesses can testify from a third-person perspective without much loss.

If we apply this conceptualization to artists, then the following, not altogether coherent, picture emerges. An artist is a moral witness, even a paradigmatic moral witness, if he or she possesses "knowledge-by-acquaintance of suffering," that is, in order to qualify as a moral witness, an artist has to have the actual and personal experience of suffering caused by an evil regime. In the absence of such experience, an artist can be a moral witness if he or she is at personal risk, either because he or she belongs to the same group of people which is targeted or because he or she tries to document what happens, or both. This documentation envisions future use, but not any use; rather, future use has to be coupled with a moral purpose, ultimately addressing a moral community, present or future. The emphasis on future use is difficult to reconcile with testimony's noninstrumentality: the testimony of a moral witness is intrinsically valuable; it is an end in itself. It is intrinsically valuable although, or because, it is not dependent on factual truth. Reporting factual truth is what political witnesses do; moral witnesses testify to what it felt like to be subjected to evil. Such testimony possesses intrinsic value independent of the question of whether it is factually correct or not. Thus, journalists, owing to their dedication to factual truth, would seem to be inclined toward the subject position of a political witness; artists, on the other hand, might be expected to be closer to the subject position of a moral witness because works of art do not normally claim factual accuracy. Indeed, as Bennett (2005:3) explains, with regard to works of art "faithful translation of testimony" is not what matters; rather, what matters is art's use of its "unique capacities to contribute actively to [the] politics [of testimony]." There is, however, an overlap between the political witness and the moral witness.

The artist as witness and intermediary

Elsewhere, I analyzed Botelho's work in light of the question of what it does to transform spectators into participant witnesses who self-critically engage with a work of art and the conditions depicted in it, including their own involvement in and responsibility for these conditions (Möller 2013:155–160). In the present article, I am interested in both reading Botelho's work in light of Margalit's understanding of the moral witness and thinking about Margalit's understanding of the moral witness in light of Botelho's works of art. Obviously, Botelho does not qualify as a paradigmatic moral witness as he does not possess *knowledge-by-acquaintance of suffering*. It is precisely the lack of such knowledge that motivated his work on the colonial wars in the first place. But observers can suffer, and they can be moral witnesses, too, on the conditions outlined earlier. To begin with, then, I need to make two alterations in Margalit's concept extending what it means to be a witness. First, I want to detach his concept from cases of *unmitigated evil* and suggest that it be used to theorize any political regime inflicting major suffering on people. I have three reasons for doing so. I am not an expert on the religious and philosophical background from which Margalit derives his understanding of unmitigated evil; I think that his concept is too important to limit its application to such cases; and I am interested in the question of what we can learn about cases of lesser evil when we look at them through approaches and concepts developed in connection with the unmitigated evil of the Holocaust. Remember that the Holocaust nowadays serves as the model for memory construction in other cases as well (Wieviorka); concepts developed in light of the Holocaust should therefore have some relevance also in connection with cases other than the Holocaust. Secondly, I want to challenge Margalit's emphasis on *contemporaneity*. Such a challenge is in accordance with recent writings in the humanities and social sciences decoupling the act of witnessing from presence on location when something happens to which a person subsequently testifies from own experience.

The risk element of Margalit's concept is probably the most difficult one when applied to Botelho's work. Taking risks is essential for the moral witness; Botelho, however, avoided risks.[21] Yet, he was supposed to be exposed to the risks and dangers of "the men of [his] generation" (Botelho) and thus to some extent "belong[ed] to the category of people toward whom the evil deeds are directed" (Margalit). That he avoided risks disqualifies him as a moral witness, although it can be argued that his work documents what happened for some future use. Without risk-taking, however, an artist cannot be a moral witness. As an artist, he cannot be a political witness, either, because the core of political witnessing is dedication to factual truth. But dedication to factual truth is not what art is about.

If we think about Botelho's work in light of the terms suggested by Margalit, then the following picture emerges. As stated above, Botelho does not qualify as a paradigmatic moral witness. He does not have the actual and personal experience of the suffering he engages with in his work. He did not take personal risks during the wars; on the contrary, he avoided such risks. Risk avoidance indeed triggered his engagement, or even obsession, with the colonial wars. However, he belongs to the generation that was made to suffer (and make others suffer) in the wars and he artistically engages with what happened for present and future use. He does so, not as a journalist in search of factual truth but as an artist. Arguably, he is not primarily interested in what it was like but in what it felt like; the texts incorporated into his drawings have an affective and emotional dimension irreconcilable with the mere reporting of facts. His is an artist's work, not a journalist's or historian's work. While the texts reproduced in the artworks may have an intrinsic value as testimonies of people who endured suffering, Botelho seems to share the hope, specified by Danchev (2009:3) as regards the artist as moralist, "that there is, or will be, an audience of sentient spectators, viewers, readers, absorbed in the work: a community, a moral community, for whom it stands up and who will stand up for it." "Witnesses," Margalit (2004:181) concludes, "are vital not just for enlarging the scope of observational knowledge but even more for elucidating the significance of human actions, symbolic acts,

[21] The young men of his generation who actually fought the war are also said to have been "disillusioned and unwilling to take risks" (Chabal 2002:14).

37

his work is vital: it can serve as an intermediary between moral witnesses and the moral community, present and future, enabling the members of this community to move along the trajectory from "what it is like" to "what it feels like" which, however, is unattainable for those who did not personally participate in the wars.

Conclusion

Artists—in contrast to photojournalists—often arrive on location only after an event or they might prefer altogether to avoid the location where something, usually something tragic, happened. They—and their works of art—nevertheless qualify (i.e., they are socially-discursively constructed) as witnesses not only of the aftermath of this event (which would be in accordance with the conventional understanding of being a witness) but also of the original event. It affects our, the recipients', understanding of what happened. Art does not necessarily produce new knowledge in an academic, scholarly sense but it "articulates a vision of the world that is insightful and consequential" (Danchev 2009:4). Recipients of works of art also become witnesses, distant witnesses, remote in space and time, not only of the work of art and that which it depicts but also of the original event referenced in the artwork, an event without which the artwork would not exist. Thus, testimony can be transferred from one person to another—from an artist to a spectator; this transfer transforms the beholder of an artwork into a witness of the original event referenced in the artwork.

Furthermore, such an artist as Manuel Botelho, without being himself a moral witness as defined by Margalit, can be an intermediary between the moral witness and the moral community, present and future, helping the members of this community to make the move from what it *is* like to what it *feels* like. Texts from original letters embedded in the artworks do not only increase the artworks' having-been-there-ness but also link their future use to what Rothberg (2009:203) calls "re-forming" of what qualifies as public and political. Such re-forming can be seen as an ingredient of the moral-political tasks of the witness when giving testimony for future use, in particular in political circumstances that favor silence—"Why the hell doesn't anyone talk about this?" (Antunes 2012:79)—rather than engagement. [22] Finally, even

[22] For example, the first major exhibition in Portugal dedicated to retornados (Portuguese people who returned from the colonies to Portugal after the independence wars) took place more than 40 years after these wars (RETORNAR: Traços de Memória, Galeria Av. da Índia, Lisbon, November 4, 2015–February 29, 2016). Likewise, it took almost 40 years to transform the former Aljube prison in Lisbon into a museum. In its original condition, the former prison, operated during the Estado novo by the political police, was open to the public in 2011 at the occasion of the exhibition Aljube—a voz das vítimas.

38

material objects such as diaries can be witnesses: they were on location when something happened; they testify from own experience; they do so for future use; and they are social agents. None of the above devalues Margalit's understanding of a moral witness. It shows, however, that extending our understanding of what it means to be a witness and decoupling it from co-presence and contemporaneity will enlarge "the scope of observational knowledge" (Margalit) and thus help better understand such highly complex and ambivalent forms of social interaction as independence wars.

References

Afonso, Aniceto, and Carlos de Matos Gomes. (2010) *Os Anos da Guerra Colonial — 1961–1975*. Lisbon and Matosinhos, Portugal: QuidNovi.

Agamben, Giorgio. (2002) *Remnants of Auschwitz: The Witness and the Archive. Translated by Daniel Heller-Roazen.* New York: Zone Books.

Antunes, António Lobo. (2008) *Knowledge of Hell.* Translated by Clifford E. Landers. Champaign, London and Dublin: Dalkey Archive Press.

Antunes, António Lobo. (2012) *The Land at the End of the World.* Translated by Margaret Jull Costa. New York/London: W.W. Norton & Company.

Azoulay, Ariella. (2014) *Infra-Destructure. In The Violence of the Image: Photography and International Conflict.* Edited by Liam Kennedy and Caitlin Patrick, 125–138. London/New York: I.B. Tauris.

Bennett, Jill. (2005) *Empathic Vision: Affect, Trauma, and Contemporary Art.* Stanford: Stanford University Press.

Bleiker, Roland. (2009) *Aesthetics and World Politics.* Houndmills: Palgrave Macmillan.

Camões, Luís Vaz de. (2001) *The Lusíads. Translated with an Introduction and Notes by Landeg White.* Oxford: Oxford University Press.

Cann, John P. (2012) *Counterinsurgency in Africa: The Portuguese Way of War 1961–1974.* Sulihull: Helion.

Chabal, Patrick. (2002) *Lusophone Africa in Historical and Comparative Perspective. In A History of Postcolonial Lusophone Africa.* Edited by Patrick Chabal with David Birmingham, Joshua Forrest, Malyn Newitt, Gerhard Seibert, and Elisa Silva Andrade, 3–134. Bloomington and Indianapolis: Indiana University Press.

Couto, Mia. (2008) *Under the Frangipani*. Translated by David Brookshaw. London: Serpent's Tail.

Danchev, Alex. (2009) *On Art and War and Terror*. Edinburgh: Edinburgh University Press.

Fujii, Lee Ann. (2009) *Killing Neighbors: Webs of Violence in Rwanda*. Ithaca/London: Cornell University Press.

Gilgen, Peter. (2003) History After Film. In Mapping *Benjamin: The Work of Art in the Digital Age*. Edited by Hans Ulrich Gumbrecht and Michael Marrinan, 53–62. Stanford: Stanford University Press.

Graham, Philip. (2009) *The Moon, Come to Earth: Dispatches from Lisbon*. Chicago/London: The University of Chicago Press.

Korhonen, Kuisma. (2008) Narrating the Trauma: Georges Perec's W ou le souvenir d'enfance. In *Terror and the Arts: Artistic, Literary, and Political Interpretations of Violence from Dostoyevsky to Abu Ghraib*. Edited by Matti Hyvärinen and Lisa Muszynski, 113–128. New York/Houndmills: Palgrave Macmillan.

LaCapra, Dominick. (1998) *History and Memory after Auschwitz*. Ithaca/London: Cornell University Press.

Laranjeiro, Catarina. (2014) Etnografia visual da Guerra Colonial. Luta de libertação na Guiné. In *O Império da Visão: Fotografia no Contexto Colonial Português (1860– 1960)*. Edited by Filipa Lowndes Vicente, 435–446. Lisbon, Portugal: Edições 70.

Levi, Primo. (1989) *The Drowned and the Saved*. Translated by Raymond Rosenthal. New York: Vintage.

Lindroos, Kia, and Frank Möller. (Forthcoming) Witnessing in Contemporary Art and Politics. In *Art as a Political Witness*. Edited by Kia Lindroos and Frank Möller. Leverkusen-Opladen, Germany: Barbara Budrich Publishers.

Lowe, Paul. (2014) The Forensic Turn: Bearing Witness and the "Thingness" of the Photograph. In *The Violence of the Image: Photography and International Conflict*. Edited by Liam Kennedy and Caitlin Patrick, 211–234. London/New York: I.B. Tauris.

Patrick, Caitlin. (2014) Ruins and Traces: Exhibiting Conflict in Guy Tillim's Leopold and Mobuto. In *The Violence of the Image: Photography and International Conflict*. Edited by Liam Kennedy and Caitlin Patrick, 235–255. London/New York: I.B. Tauris.

Pessoa, Fernando. (1996) *The Book of Disquietude by Bernardo Soares, Assistant Book Keeper in the City of Lisbon*. Translated with an Introduction by Richard Zenith. Revised paperback edition. Manchester: Carcanet.

Piçarra, Maria do Carmo. (2014) Azuis ultramarinos: Imagens-clarão do colonialismo português no cinema. In *Imagens coloniais: Revelações da antropologia e da arte contemporânea*. Edited by Nuno Faria, 71–96. Guimarães, Portugal: Centro Internacional das Artes José de Guimarães.

Porfírio, José Luís. (2010) Manuel Botelho — Aerograms for 2010. In *Professores*. Edited by Isabel Carlos, 71–76. Lisbon, Portugal: Centro de Arte Moderna, Fundação Calouste Gulbenkian.

Ramos, Afonso. (2014) Angola 1961, o horror das imagens. In *O Império da Visão: Fotografia no Contexto Colonial Português (1860 – 1960)*. Edited by Filipa Lowndes Vicente, 399–434. Lisbon, Portugal: Edições 70.

Roberts, John. (2014) *Photography and Its Violations*. New York: Columbia University Press.

Rothberg, Michael. (2009) *Multidirectional Memory: Remembering the Holocaust in the Age of Decolonization*. Stanford: Stanford University Press.

Shapiro, Michael J. (2009) *Cinematic Geopolitics*. New York/London: Routledge.

Simpson, David. (2006) *9/11: The Culture of Commemoration*. Chicago/London: The University of Chicago Press.

Struck, Janina. (2011) *Private Pictures: Soldiers' Inside View of War*. London/New York: I.B. Tauris.

Venter, Al J. (2015) *Portugal e as Guerrilhas de África: As guerras portuguesas em Angola, Moçambique e Guiné Portuguesa 1961–1974*. Lisbon, Portugal: Clube de Autor.

Vicente, Filipa Lowndes, ed. (2014) *O Império da Visão: Fotografia no Contexto Colonial Português (1860 – 1960)*. Lisbon, Portugal: Edições 70.
Wieviorka, Annette. (2006) The Era of the Witness. Translated by Jared Stark. Ithaca/London: Cornell University Press.

Winter, Jay. (1995) *Sites of Memory, Sites of Mourning: The Great War in European Cultural History*. Cambridge: Cambridge University Press.

Remember Me

Sorcha Carey

Editor's Note: *This article is adapted from the introduction to the catalogue for the 2016 Edinburgh Art Festival, UK's largest celebration of visual art. The essay references art installations at the 2016 Art Festival. The author is the Director of the Edinburgh Art Festival and author of* Pliny's Catalogue of Culture: Art and Empire in the Natural History.

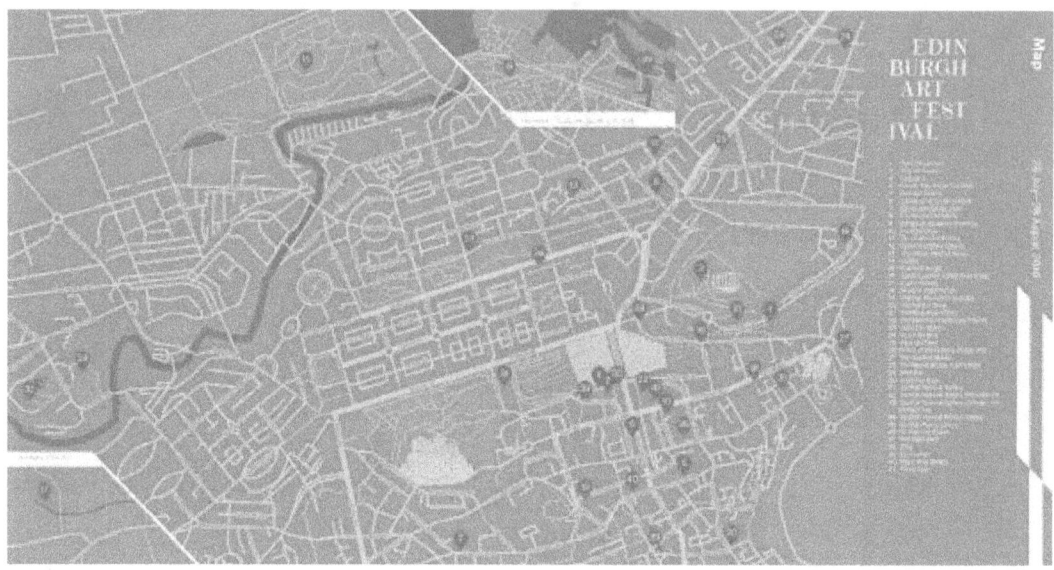

Image courtesy of the Edinburgh Art Festival

Remember Me

Our cities are filled with monuments: the material evidence of a profoundly human urge to memorialise, as well as a constantly evolving archive of who and what has mattered to previous generations.

The word has its origins in the Latin verb *monere*, meaning 'to remind, warn, advise'; from the first, carving out a proactive instructional role for monuments. Though if two recent encounters are anything to go by, it seems that increasingly, monuments are losing their inherent authority. A small sign spotted on a recent visit to Naples made the following entreaty: *Cittadini. Rispettare i suoi monumenti* ('Citizens! Respect your monuments!').

While, closer to home, the World War I memorial on Edinburgh's Royal Mile, is accompanied by a sign advising visitors to *'Please Respect the War Memorial'*.

If the Romans have given us the word for monument, then they also understood that a monument was not necessarily a guarantee of memory. Over two millennia ago, the poet Horace opened his *Ode 3.30* with the claim that, with something as apparently ephemeral as a poem, he had *'built a monument more lasting than bronze'*. Implicit in Horace's poem is a knowing sense that it is neither material nor environment that determine whether a monument will last: the longevity of a monument is directly dependent on the reception it receives.

The Romans regularly engaged in what modern scholars have termed *damnatio memoriae*; a set of actions deliberately intended to eradicate the memory of those who had fallen from favour, including erasing names from inscriptions, destroying statues and even demolishing an individual's house (Note 1). As long as humans have erected monuments, they have been assaulted, convenient proxies for the individual and ideas commemorated therein. The recent campaigns to remove statues of Cecil Rhodes in Cape Town and Oxford, are but the la test manifestations in a centuries-old trend.

But the fate of the vast majority of historic monuments in our cities is perhaps most accurately captured in Jonathan Owen's *Eraser Drawings* (statues), (2008-9). With painstaking precision, and using nothing more than an eraser, Owen re-worked a series of photographic reproductions taken from books on public statues, to render the figures invisible. Literally re-forming the statues into the background forms they were obscuring (a park, a 1970s office block, a tree), Owen enacts the fate of many a monument, as over time, they blend into the background, becoming invisible to the contemporary eye.

Deconstructing the Monument

Owen's first publicly sited project has been specifically devised for the Burns Monument. Designed by the architect, Thomas Hamilton, to house a full-length portrait of Robert Burns by John Flaxman, the circular temple is modelled on the Choragic Monument of Lysicrates in Athens, and was completed in 1831. Just a few years later, however, the statue of Burns was removed to the Scottish National Portrait Gallery (where it remains to this day), amidst fears that smoke from a nearby gasworks would damage the sculpture.

This empty monument offers a resonant context for Owen's new work, a re-worked life-size figure of a nymph (made just a few years after the monument itself opened). In Owen's re-working, the entire torso has been re-shaped into a series of interlinked chains. Only the gentle indent of a navel on the lowest link survives, to allude to what has been removed. The work is the first female figure that Owen has worked on, and in tune with previous sculptures, his intervention re-activates the figure, drawing out truths already latent in the figure's original form. Precisely in the removal of some of the more overtly sexual qualities of the figure (the breasts, the curve of the waist), Owen lays bare the strategies of the original sculpture. Her head collapsed, her body disjointed, the nymph appears eroded and collapsed by two centuries of the male gaze.

There are very few women represented in Edinburgh's impressive collection of monuments (indeed there are almost as many representations of animals as women). And while the female form was a mainstay of nineteenth century memorials, it was most often chosen as a cipher to embody abstract ideas and ideals – whether 'justice', the 'genius of architecture', or, in the case of Owen's nymph, as a repository for male fantasy. The original statue which provides the raw material for Owen's contemporary re-working, as well as the setting in which it is located, speak the classic language of monuments, invoking the architecture of gods to confer immortality on the individual commemorated. But in Owen's playful deconstruction, the artist invites us to reflect not on an individual, but on who and what we immortalise.

Lost Monuments

Bani Abidi has long been interested in the forms and materials of remembering. Her film installation, *Death at a 30 degree angle*, (2012), explores the efforts of a politician to ensure his memory is preserved for posterity. Abidi's film follows him as he visits the studio of the monumental sculptor who has been commissioned to portray him and attempts to identify the costume and gesture which will best secure him a place in the annals. The irony, of course, is the absolute redundancy of the idiom, as we remember the endless monumental portraits of communist leaders, overthrown dictators or imperial functionaries, languishing in storage around the world.

Her new work, *Memorial to Lost Words*, draws on the more ephemeral medium of sound to reflect on things which have not been commemorated in the

46

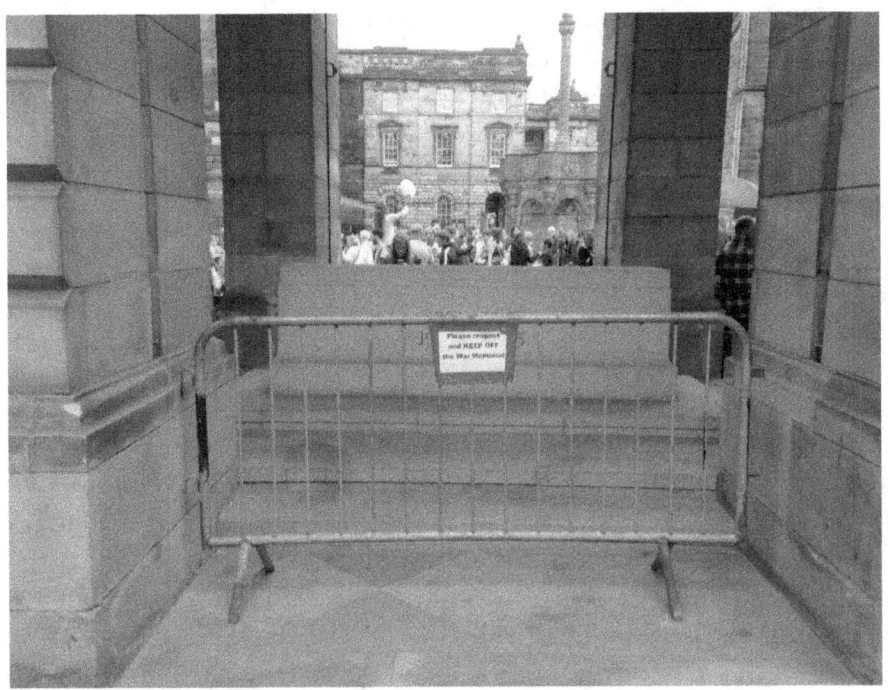

Image Courtesy of Edinburgh Art Festival

official records, or indeed which have been deliberately expunged. More than one million Indian soldiers served in the British Army during the First World War. And while the common (mis)conception is one of noble sacrifice made by Sikh soldiers, extending a warrior tradition into the service of empire, Abidi's sound installation explores an alternative history.

Memorial to Lost Words fills the debating chamber of Edinburgh's New Parliament House with two sets of voices, singing in dialogue. The rest are those of women singing folk songs in Punjabi, entreating their menfolk not to go to war. Archived by the poet Amarjit Chandan, and now re-recorded by the artist working with contemporary folk singers, the songs were first sung 100 years ago.

In response, we hear a newly composed folk song, based on letters (now in the British Library) written by Indian soldiers to their wives and families from the front. Filled with honest descriptions of the brutality and absurdity of war, the letters were censored and many never reached their intended recipients.

Abidi's work gives voice to stories which have been excluded from the official record, as well as mainstream historical accounts. But it also celebrates less monumental forms of memory. The folk song is a profoundly oral and embodied tradition, dependent for its survival on regular performance by successive generations. While Chandan's archive has preserved these voices on paper, Abidi's sound installation brings them back to life. Crafted from discarded memories (deliberate and accidental), Abidi's memorial reminds us that like Horace's ode, the apparently transient and ephemeral can far outlast the royal tombs of kings.

Living Monuments

In the period immediately following the Second World War, as countries around the world erected monuments to their dead, New Zealand's government took the decision not to commission new cenotaphs or statues. Instead, alongside adding the names of the dead to existing memorials, they would erect 'living monuments': utilitarian buildings intended to provide space for communities to come together and grow. Olivia Webb took inspiration from these 'living monuments' in developing her *Voices Project* (2014), working with communities who had lost their places of worship in the aftermath of two devastating earthquakes which struck the city of Christchurch in September 2010 and February 2011.

Webb formed a choir in three affected communities, and over the course of a month, the choirs (whose members had little or no prior experience of singing Classical music) met regularly to learn Thomas Tallis' sixteenth century motet, *If Ye Love Me*. The resulting sound installation, installed on the sites of each of the demolished churches, reflected the entire development of the project, from mingling to warm-up to rehearsal and performance; embodying not a single moment of perfection, but a process of learning, testing and sharing. Less a commemoration of things lost, and more a memorial to those things gained through the sharing of loss, the *Voices Project* is a monument to new communities in the very moment of their formation.

Re-developed for *More Lasting than Bronze*, Webb's sound installation fills the Renaissance architecture of Edinburgh's Trinity Apse with the voices of unseen people. Originally built as Trinity College Kirk in 1460, and demolished in 1848 to make way for the railway, some of the surviving elements of the original structure (including the choir) were rebuilt as Trinity Apse in the

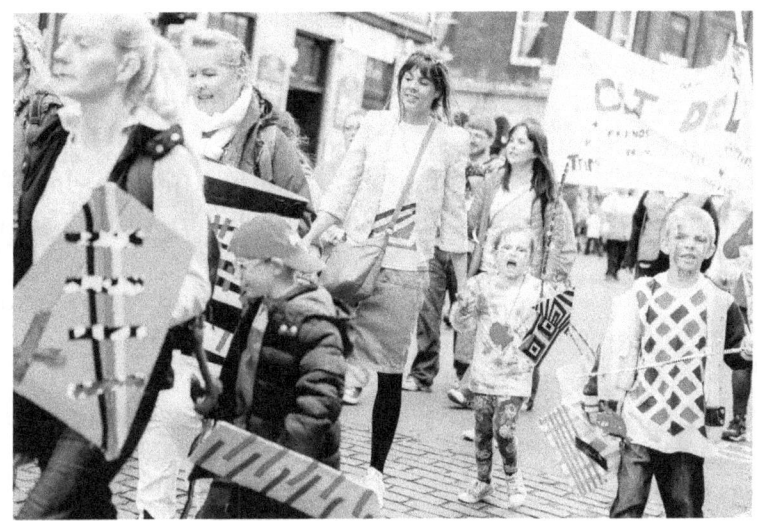

Image Courtesy of Edinburgh Art Festival

1870s. With its own history of destruction and displacement, the building provides a fitting context for the *Voices Project*.

Webb is interested in the way in which architecture can act as a reservoir for memory, accumulating the unseen residues of the actions, words, and thoughts that it has enclosed. The *Voices Project* arose directly from the loss of these solid architectural forms, and with them, the memories and social histories they had shaped and contained. In a new choral project, *Lapides Vivi (Living Stones)*, Webb will establish a choir for the duration of the festival, to explore the relationship between lives lived and the stones which have embraced them.

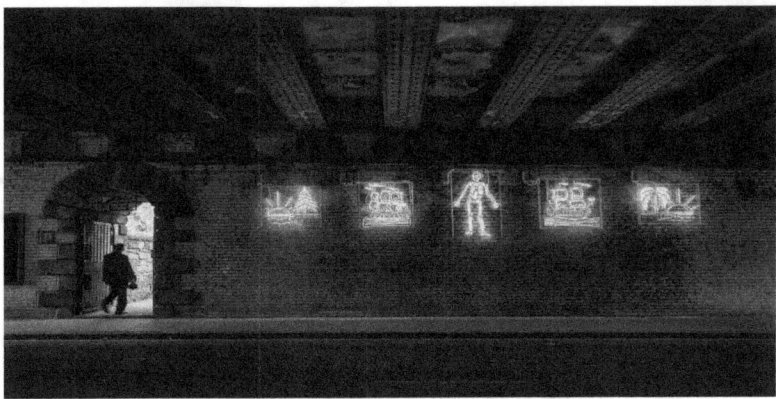

Image Courtesy of Edinburgh Art Festival

Missing Monuments

One of the few women to be remembered with a monument in Edinburgh is the children's author and philanthropist, Catherine Sinclair (1800-1864). Designed by John Rhind, the monument was erected in 1868, and the accompanying inscription remembers Sinclair as 'the friend of all children', as well as the person responsible for Edinburgh's first drinking fountain.

Sally Hackett's *The Fountain of Youth*, playfully reinterprets a monumental form to reflect on the absence of monuments to young people in our cities. Made with the direct involvement of children from Tollcross Primary School, Hackett's fountain is encased in colourful ceramic forms. Ceramic is not a material usually associated with traditional monuments, which have preferred to look to more expensive materials to commemorate their subjects. It has however long been used in outdoor shrines, perhaps most famously in those produced by Andrea Della Robbia (1435-1525) at the height of the Florentine Renaissance.

It is a fitting material, then, for a work which plays on contemporary society's cult of youth and celebrity. Hackett's *The Fountain of Youth* gives contemporary expression to a human desire documented as far back as the 5th century bce, when the Greek historian Herodotus recorded reports of a miraculous fountain in the Land of the Macrobians, guaranteeing long-life and youthful appearance to anyone who drank from it (Note 2). The irony is that while contemporary media may idolise youth (at the same time as promoting a whole host of serums and creams which promise to help us to retain it), our monuments still tend to honour individuals of more advanced years.

Hackett's fountain is installed in the courtyard garden of the Museum of Edinburgh, formerly Huntly House, also known as 'The Speaking House', for the series of advisory inscriptions mounted on its façade. These include the customary reminders of human mortality (*Today for me, tomorrow for thee, why worry?*) as well as one more recent and more optimistic inscription, added when the building was restored in 1932: *'I am old but renew my youth'*. Hackett's playful sculpture is a tting addition to these *memento mori* – a humorous reflection on contemporary society, but also a reminder to remember future generations as much as looking to the past.

Monument to Experience

Installed in the shadow of Calton Hill with its many classical monuments which earned Edinburgh the title 'The Athens of the North', Graham Fagen's new work, *A Drama in Time*, is a monument to everyman, celebrating not the lofty achievements of a single individual, but the lived experience of mankind.

Consisting of five emblematic images made in neon, Fagen's light installation sits at the foot of Jacob's Ladder, a steep set of steps leading from the Old Town up to Calton Hill, named after the stairway connecting earth with heaven which, according to the Book of Genesis, Jacob witnessed in a dream. Weaving in a rich set of references to its surrounding locale, Fagen's new work presents a symbolic journey through life, from birth to death.

At the centre of Fagen's installation, framed by rising and setting suns, stands a skeleton, an abstract representation of man, as much as a reminder of our own mortality. On either side of the central figure are two ships, communicating a sense of a journey, but also a reference to the poet, Robert Burns, commemorated in the monument at the top of the steps. On several occasions, struggling to earn a living through his poetry, Burns had considered sailing to the West Indies to take up a position on a sugar plantation. In 2006 Fagen made a series of screen-prints of three ships on which Burns had booked passage but never sailed: The Bell, Nancy and The Roselle. The neon ships in *A Drama in Time* are modelled on these earlier works, and remind us of the paths not taken, as much as the roads travelled.

Fagen's installation borrows its title from the visionary town planner and key figure in the conservation of Edinburgh's Old Town, Patrick Geddes, who remarked, '*A city is more than a place in space, it is a drama in time*'. Geddes advocated a holistic approach to the development of cities, believing in observation, and lessons gained through experience: his motto was '*by living we learn*'. Fagen's neons (a material commonly used in shops signs and advertising) speak the language of the everyday in their form as much as their content. Drawings in light, they remember remember not the feats of heroes, but the forces that shape us, and the lived, often haphazard, experience of ordinary life. lived, often haphazard, experience of ordinary life.

Encoded Monument

If a monument is '*anything that preserves memory of a person or an event*' (Note 3), then Ciara Phillips' *Every Woman* can quite rightly be described as one, and at 75 metres long, it is certainly 'monumental'. The work is Phillips' response to the 'dazzle designs' widely applied to ships in the latter part of the First World War, in an effort to afford some protection against an increasingly successful German U-Boat campaign. The artist Norman Wilkinson is credited with 'inventing' the technique, which involved covering ships in strong optical designs and bold colour contrasts.

In researching the technique, Phillips was immediately drawn to a photograph of the studio established in London's Royal Academy to generate designs for ships. Almost everyone in the image is a woman. While the role of women in the Second World War is quite widely documented, the history of women in the First World War is still largely untold. This despite the fact that, as part of the war e ort, women regularly took up roles which had traditionally been the preserve of men, working, for example, as tram drivers, telegraphists and dazzle designers.

Phillips has covered the entire surface of the MV Fingal with a bold gestural design characteristic of her practice based in printmaking – indeed, the design is a reworked and enlarged version of a screen-printed scarf the artist made in 2013. Overlaid on the surface of the design, at the ship's stern, is a message in Morse Code, which reads: Every Woman a Signal Tower. The text reworks the title of James Spratt's *The Homograph or Every Man a Signal Tower*, first published in 1808, in which the author described how with a simple handkerchief, anyone could use their body to transmit messages across long distances.

Ciara Phillips' *Every Woman* signals a different form for the monument – a monument which is not about preserving for posterity the inspired invention of a single individual, but which reflects on the collective and largely unacknowledged endeavours of women in the First World War. *Every Woman* is a clarion call, a plea to embody and keep alive memory through our actions and thinking. A reminder that the female body is no cipher for externally imposed ideals, but a bearer of its own unique messages. Then and now, every woman, Phillips reminds us, has something to signal.

Scan here to watch a timelapse video of Ciara Phillips' *Every Woman*

http://bit.ly/2izMcxe

Contested Monuments

In 1968 a small plaque was erected on Edinburgh's Cowgate to commemorate James Connolly, born there, exactly one hundred years before. Shortly after, the plaque was stolen. And though a replacement remains safely there to this day, the initial theft is testament to the extent to which Connolly's memory has been contested from the moment of his execution on the 12th May 1916 for his role in Ireland's Easter Rising.

Roderick Buchanan's new film explores the complex relationship between Edinburgh and its socialist and revolutionary son. *Understanding versus Sympathy* is, in the artist's words, 'a shadow portrait'; an exploration of Connolly's life as viewed through the lens of the Irish historian and Edinburgh resident, Owen Dudley Edwards. Connolly was born and raised in extreme poverty in Edinburgh in 1868, ultimately moving to Ireland in 1910 to work for the Irish Transport and General Workers Union. Owen Dudley Edwards was born and raised in Dublin, before moving to Edinburgh to take up a position at the university.

Buchanan's film focuses on the captivating face and voice of Dudley Edwards, as he speaks about the life and times of James Connolly. Dudley Edwards has a strong professional interest in Connolly, having written several books on the Easter Rising and its wider historical context. But he also has a strong personal connection with the period. He recounts, for example, how his own grandfather attended a lecture by Arthur Griffiths (founder of Sinn Féin) and on attempting to ask a question, was promptly rebuffed by Griffiths for being an Englishman. *Understanding versus Sympathy* offers an extended reflection on different forms of memory, as Dudley Edwards' commentary weaves seamlessly from erudite historical observation to personal remembrance.

Scan here to watch an interview with
Ciara Phillips

https://vimeo.com/168048090

Filmed against a stark black background, the film has a statuesque quality, at times making Dudley Edwards appear as if a monument come to life. But in the complexities of its central character (Dudley Edwards) and subject (Connolly), Understanding versus Sympathy emerges not as a portrait of Dudley Edwards, or memorial to James Connolly; more as an extended reflection on monuments themselves, as carefully crafted projections in stone of just one aspect (deliberately chosen, and, at the time, apparently certain) in a set of complex, ever-shifting, awkward truths.

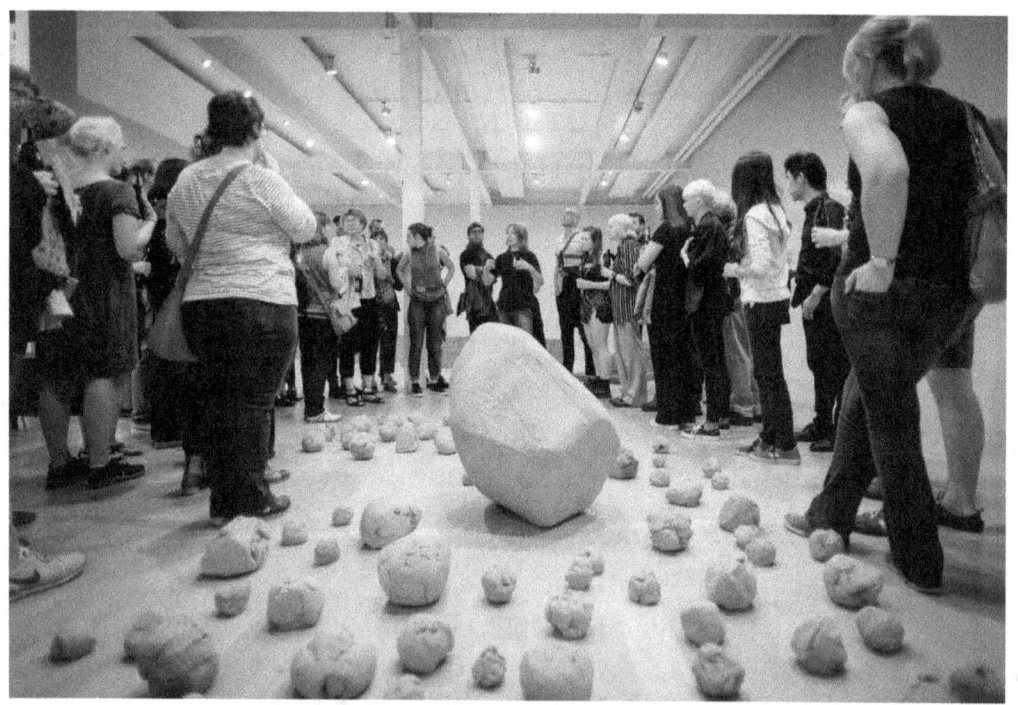

Image Courtesy of Edinburgh Art Festival

Notes

1.   Eric R. Varner. (2004). *Mutilation and Transformation: Damnatio Memoriae and Roman Imperial Portraiture* (Monumenta Graeca et Romana, 10). Leiden.

2.   Herodotus. *The Histories*, Book 3.23

3.   Definition of monument in the *Chambers Dictionary 12th Edition*, London, 2011.

Theme 2:

Participation + Hierarchy

Curating Public Art 2.0: The Case of *Autopoiesis*

Btihaj Ajana

Btihaj Ajana is a Senior Lecturer in Culture, Digital Humanities, and Creative Industries at King's College London. She is also a Marie Curie Research Fellow and Associate Professor at the Aarhus Institute of Advanced Studies. She is the author of Governing through Biometrics: The Biopolitics of Identity *(2013).*

Abstract

This article examines the intersections between public art, curation and Web 2.0 technology. Building on the case study of Autopoiesis, a digital art project focusing on the curation and online exhibition of artworks received from members of the public in the United Arab Emirates, the article explores the ways and extent to which a Web platform can enable participatory culture and novel forms of audience engagement. While major cultural institutions in the region tend to promote brand-like activities and prestige cultural projects, Autopoiesis seeks to offer a more inclusive platform to facilitate autonomous creative self-expressions and enable greater public participation in culture. By providing a critical reflection on the "material" contexts of this digital project, the article also demonstrates the related tensions between the virtual and the physical, and the wider "local" realities enframing this project.

Introduction

The domain of art and culture has always been a site of contention and power struggle. From issues of representation and preservation to issues of access and democratization, the cultural field remains the subject of sustained debates regarding its meaning and function in society and its role in maintaining or challenging existing structures of hierarchy and power. Questions as to whose narratives and memories are being represented in museums, who has access to cultural spaces, and who decides on what counts and qualifies as art and culture, are some of the many recurring concerns often found in debates about cultural production, preservation, and transmission. Crucial to these debates is also the concept of curating which has long been an important and fundamental feature in cultural and museum processes, given the curator's active and performative role in the overall production of meaning, memory, and knowledge, and in animating the encounter between past, present, and future.

Over the last few years, the function and practice of curating both inside and outside museums have undergone a number of transformations due to a host of factors, some of which have to do with the challenges and opportunities brought about by globalization, while others are directly related to the advent of digital and Web 2.0 technologies and their growing deployment within cultural institutions. As Cairns and Birchall (2013) argue, museums are increasingly required to share "the authority of meaning-making" with their audiences and other communities. Finding new methods of curating objects (material and digital) and communicating meaning has thus become a necessary task for cultural institutions.

The aim of this article is to explore the curatorial potential (and limitations) of Web 2.0 in light of its networked affordances and the user-driven participatory culture it claims to enable. By networked affordances we mean the possibilities of interaction and creation that are facilitated through the intersection of technologies, practices, and different publics. Or to borrow a definition from Cabiddu et al. (2014:176), the concept of affordance, in the context of digital media forms, designates the "symbiotic relationship between human activities and technological capabilities", providing a language for examining the impact of technological tools and platforms on various social and creative practices. As such, and by examining the affordances of Web 2.0 in relation to public art and curatorial practice, this article contributes to the body of literature engaging with affordance theory and to the fields of curatorial studies, media studies, and digital culture. The value of this work lies primarily in its multidisciplinary and exploratory approach to the issue of curating as well its empirical and reflective engagement with a specific site of inquiry, namely the example of the digital platform, *Autopoiesis* (www.autopoiesis.io).

Autopoiesis is a public art project supported by the Cultural Institute at King's College London and led by the author of this article. It focuses on the interplay between curation, participation and ethics, especially with regard to the role of digital platforms in facilitating more participatory and democratic forms of cultural and audience engagement. Taking the United Arab Emirates (UAE) as the background of its inquiry, the project seeks to collect, curate, and display an online selection of artwork received from members of the public who are from, living in or transiting through the UAE.

The project considers the idea of curating as a "digital activity" (Cairns and Birchall 2013) whose task is/ought to be primarily about the normative act of *enabling*; enabling wider representations and more diverse voices within the process of cultural praxis, "prosumption" and exhibition, through the use of Web 2.0 technologies as a tool to "decentralize authority" (Shahani et al. 2008:4). Traditionally, curation has been partly about the act of selection which is linked to what Cairns and Birchall (2013) refers to as "the core requirement of deciding what of a culture to keep, and how best to do so". However, selection and exclusion often go hand in hand insofar as selection inevitably involves demarcating the lines between what is deemed worthy of preservation and transmission and what is not, and acting as a filter of "cultural abundance" (ibid.). It is through selection that curators and institutions derive their authority and power, and with it the ability to include and exclude.

In his discussion on emergent curatorial models and the role of electronic technology, the media artist and theorist Patrick Lichty (2003:1) argues that "the legitimization of the work or the institution itself does not [traditionally] come from populist or democratic impulses, but from oligarchic materialist practices originated with the birth of the museum". Therefore, traditional models of curation that rest on mainstream museum practices are often monopolistic and hierarchal. But with the advent of the Internet, Lichty argues, the top-down approach to cultural production and the centrality of museum practices are increasingly being challenged through alternative curatorial efforts and Web-based cultural and artistic practices.

Correlatively, *Autopoiesis* project represents an attempt to explore alternatives to the power-driven and institutionally embedded processes of traditional curation by engaging with the notion of curating as a participatory digital activity, not only theoretically but also from a practice-based perspective. The aim of the project has been to test the extent to which digital curation can offer, potentially at least, "new spaces for autonomous producers and DIY culture", as Paul (quoted in Krysa 2006:17) suggests, and allow a greater public engagement with cultural production and curatorial processes. Underlying the project is also the related issue of ethics, an issue that remains inextricably linked to processes of curation and cultural production and representation. In fact and at its very basic etymological level, the very meaning of the word "curating" goes back to the Latin term "cura", meaning "care" and "cure", which is evocative of the ethical and normative dimension of the curatorial role (see also Martinon 2013). In the context of *Autopoiesis*, the ethical aspect of this project lies in its ambition to create a public platform that is participatory, inclusive and engaging beyond the constraining walls of official institutions.

In what follows, I shall begin with a more detailed discussion on the background and objectives of the project followed by an examination of the ethnographic landscape of the UAE, which represents the backdrop for *Autopoiesis*. I will then move on to discuss at some length some aspects, advantages, and limitations of digitally mediated art platforms, particularly in relation to issues of public participation and access. In addition, the article also provides a reflection on the "materiality" of the digital and the related tensions between the virtual and the physical, which prompt the need to attend to the local realities and material contexts of digital projects and platforms.

Autopoiesis

"Autopoiesis", which literally means the act of "self-creation and self-production", is an evocative metaphor for what this art project aims to achieve, that is, to provide people from all walks of life, who are living in or visiting the UAE, with the opportunity to create and exhibit their own artwork that is expressive of their diverse identities, cultures, and life experiences in the region. The project invites the submission of multimedia work from artists and non-artists, with a focus on personal narrative and perspectives.

The overarching objective of the project is to offer a platform for autonomous self-expression beyond official institutions and their dominant "branding" activities manifested, for instance, in the new Abu Dhabi's Cultural District on the Saadiyat Island and its mega satellite museums. At the heart of *Autopoiesis* is the motivation to express the daily realities and complexities of the UAE culture and society and provide the viewer with a window into the personal and communal aspects of the region as experienced by its own residents and visitors regardless of their citizenship status and socio-economic background. *Autopoiesis* is therefore an experiment that seeks to reveal how different people from the UAE society think and feel about the culture and identity of the region. If they were given the chance to express and curate these themselves based on their experiences, narratives and memories, what would the picture look like? How different would it be from an "officially" curated version? As such, the project is less concerned with representing or solidifying a monolithic singular (meta-)narrative about the UAE culture and more interested in reclaiming the multiple fragments of memory and identity in all of their contradictions, complexities, pluralities, and diversities. To accomplish this, *Autopoiesis* harnesses the potential of Web 2.0 technology. To understand why this is important in the context of the UAE, it is crucial to understand first and foremost the ethnographic aspect of the UAE and the make-up of its population.

Ethnographic landscape of the UAE

The first thing that might strike any visitor to the UAE is the diverse, immigrant-rich nature of its population, something that is not always reflected in the "official" identity discourses. In fact, foreign nationals make up almost 90% of the population with South-Asian groups being the majority (almost 60%). In addressing the issue of citizenship in the UAE, the anthropologist Neha Vora describes "a triptych of identities" underpinning the population of the UAE: the "local" (native Emarati "citizens"), the "expatiate" (mainly Anglo-European nationals) and the "migrant" (primarily South Asians) (2013:31). Each of these identification categories subsumes further transnational identities adding to the complexity of the ethnographic landscape of the UAE. Importantly, these categories are by no means neutral or equal. They are highly value-laden and mobilized according to parameters of hierarchies, power, and distinctions that are set by various entities including the state and non-state institutions and groups. Questions of inclusion and exclusion are therefore inextricably linked to this triptych of identities. They are, as Vora (2013:21) explains, defined according to a dichotomy of citizen and non-citizen wherein the juridico-legal category of "Emarati" dictates the criteria for belonging, mobility, and access to state resources.

In addition, citizenship is the UAE is patrilineal, and there is not much room for naturalization (ibid.). So, those born to Emarati mothers do not become Emarati citizens. Citizenship is, as such, defined not only by ethnic origins but also by sex and gender in a way that restricts access to full civic and cultural participation and representation. At the same time, the UAE state produces "neoliberal" subjects who, through their entrepreneurial activities, can benefit from privatized rights, consumer and business-based models of quasi-citizenship. In doing so, the UAE deploys "multiple logics of citizenship", as Vora (2012:790) puts it, whereby different groups are given differential treatments, privileges, and forms of belonging according to neoliberal ethos of productivity and economic participation, in which a particular kind of foreigner is favored: the Western-educated, English speaking, middle-class expatriate.

The hierarchical structure of UAE identities and citizenship often carries over into the realm of cultural production and representation. Recently, the UAE has been receiving much international attention following the massive expansion in its museum and cultural projects. Examples include the construction of the Louvre Abu Dhabi and Guggenheim Abu Dhabi as part of the Saadiyat Island master plan whose total cost exceeds $27 billion (Davidson 2013). These emerging developments are indeed representative of the country's ambition to become a cultural hub in the Gulf region and brand itself as a progressive and open Arab country. Museums are after all "identity machines", as McClellan (2012:278) argues, and often play a significant role in cementing the notion of nationhood and staking a claim of civilization and progress.

However, this vision of promoting national identity and constructing a so-called civilized image through culture does not seem to always sit comfortably with a context where censorship exists and the class structure is heavily demarcated and racialized. Abu Dhabi has already been criticized repeatedly for the working conditions of migrant labourers building its cultural institutions. In March 2011, for instance, a petition has been launched by Gulf Labor, which more than 2,000 artists signed, calling for the boycott of Guggenheim over the treatment of migrant workers in the Saadiyat Island (see gulflabor.org). In October 2013, a coalition of international artists has launched a "52 weeks" campaign to protest against the labour conditions on the Saadiyat Island. Artists and members of the Gulf Labor have been exhibiting, on a weekly basis, artwork that highlights the living and working conditions of workers building cultural institutions in Abu Dhabi (Batty 2013; Gulf Labor n.d.). One of the active members of Gulf Labor is New

York University professor Andrew Ross who has been barred from traveling to the United Arab Emirates following his criticism of the labor conditions there (*New York Times* 2015). In May 2015, the UAE also blocked the entry of two Gulf Labor artists, Walid Raad and Ashok Sukumaran, into the country.

In addition to censorship and human labor concerns, questions are also being raised as to whether the current museum and cultural developments in the UAE are capable of fully representing the diverse identities and cultures of both the local and migrant populations in the country, and allow different individuals and groups the opportunity and space for meaningful cultural expression and engagement. One criticism that is often levelled at these developments involves their presumed bias toward Western endorsed approaches and categories over other forms of artistic expression as well as the fetishization of prestige through the globalization and use of established museum brands. Hans Ulrich Obrist (quoted in Batty 2012) captured some of these concerns when he argued that there is the danger of the "homogenizing force" of globalization, which can threaten local voices and diminish hybridity and difference if culture becomes merely an import. A similar concern is expressed by the art historian and curator Maymanah Farhat who argues that "the Emirates have poured millions of dollars into

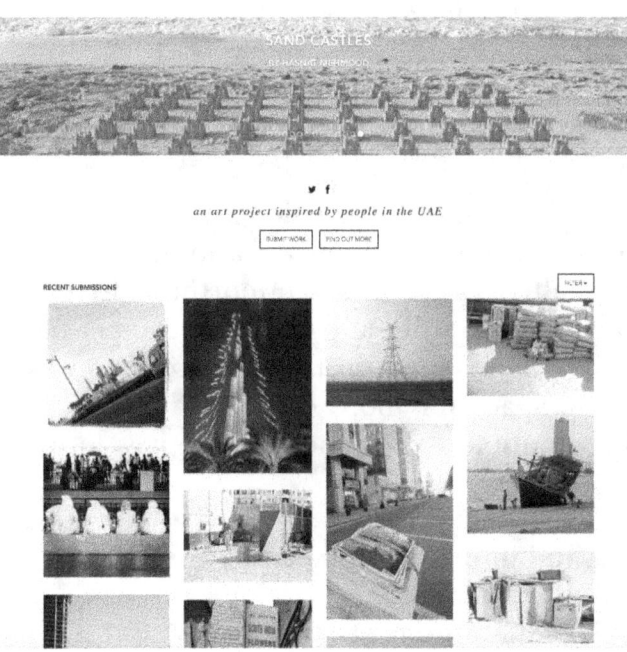

Figure 1. *Autopoiesis* display

initiatives that seek to replicate the market-driven, politically influenced arts scenes found in New York and London" (quoted in McClellan 2012:287). Homogeneity and cultural replication remain indeed recurring concerns in many current commentaries on the UAE's developing art and cultural scene.

At the heart of these concerns lies also the issue of audience access and participation. For whom are these cultural initiatives envisaged, after all? This is an important question no doubt given the interesting population structure of the UAE and its highly heterogeneous and hierarchical demographic context. For instance, one could wonder how relevant to the cultural worldview of the Indian construction worker is a branch of the Louvre managed by a well-paid French agency? To what extent museums' architectural spaces, designed to make an impact and gain prestige, might actually feel condescending and excluding for large groups of the population? How can these cultural developments reach out to wider audiences when the different segments of society, be they citizen members, wealthy diasporic elite or Bangladeshi workers, do not necessarily share same cultural points of reference? As Pierre Bourdieu (1968 [1984]) remarks, audience engagement with and appreciation of art and culture is a "trained" capacity, access to which is not always equally distributed among social strata. The cultural field is indeed by no means a flat, neutral, or equal space but one that is inextricably linked to hierarchies, distinctions, and power struggles (Ajana 2015:329).

These questions are but some of the challenging issues that lurk beneath the nascent cultural and art scene in the UAE and the wider Gulf region. At the same time, these challenges are also an opportunity to rethink the nature and function of culture and curating, and reflect on their ethical and political dimensions. It is against such a backdrop that *Autopoiesis* was conceived, in the spirit of offering a space for more open and diverse participation in culture, and allowing multiple voices and perspectives to emerge, through the affordances of Web 2.0 technologies.

Digital participation and multivocality

Central to *Autopoiesis* is the notion of the "digital" and the belief that the online environment enables opportunities of access and participation beyond material borders and the constrains of citizenship conditions in the region. Particularly, and given its dynamic and user-driven characteristics, Web 2.0 is highly relevant to the functioning and objectives of *Autopoiesis*.

64

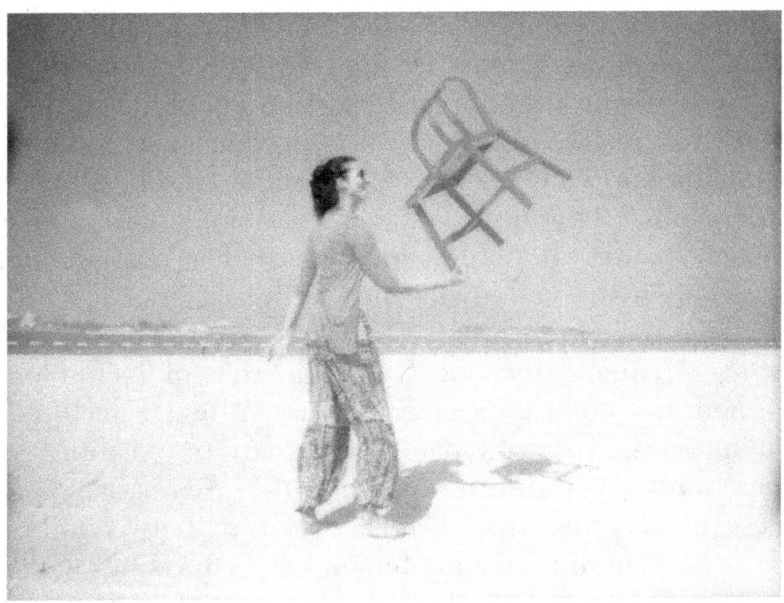

Figure 2. Sean Blake (2014): "The Untitled Chair Project" is a photography portrait series that aims to help "raise awareness for the need for registered bone marrow donors. The red chair serves as a consistent visual element that helps to tie the photos together and attract attention".

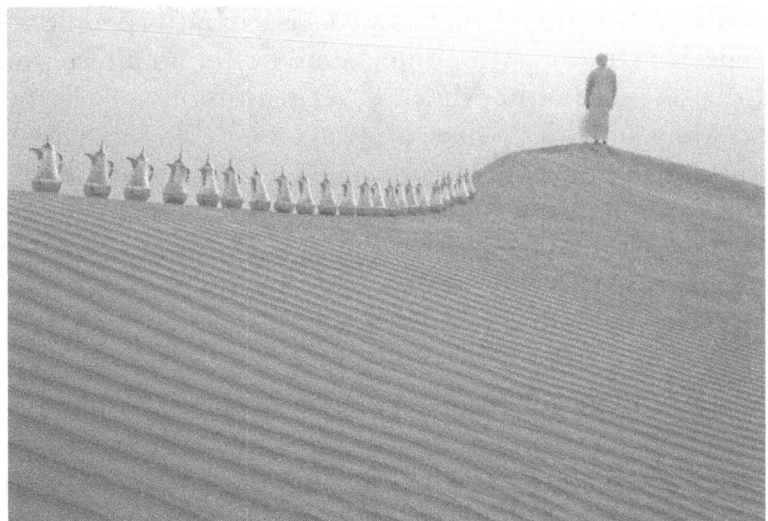

Figure 3. Hamad Al Falasi (2014): "Desert Bejewelled", a photography series capturing "the essence of hospitality in the Arabian culture by means of Arabic Coffee. The desert has always been a place of wonder. This has been further highlighted with Arabic coffee as a symbol that links the desert inhabitant with her environment."

The technology of Web 2.0 was initially popularized by Tim O'Reilly (2005) who defined it as the second generation of the World Wide Web. Compared with Web 1.0, Web 2.0 is marked by the transition from static HTML web pages to more dynamic web applications that enable users to participate, interact, share information online as well as produce user-generated content. O'Reilly explains that whereas Web 1.0 is about "publication", Web 2.0 is about "participation". Therefore, Web 2.0 technologies are often considered as highly participatory in nature and regarded as an enabling tool for grassroots and open-sourced involvement of web users.

In their study of digital museums and the role of technology, Ramesh Srinivasan and his colleagues argue that "Web 2.0 technologies have introduced increasingly participatory practices to creating content [...] reaching and engaging with new audiences" (Srinivasan et al. 2008:1). They suggest that a "growing schism is developing between grassroots ICT [Information and Communications Technology] efforts devoted to activism, participation, and cultural mobilization versus the top-down bureaucratic approaches toward digitizing cultural heritage objects" (ibid.: 1, 9). While not attempting to necessarily reinforce such schism, *Autopoiesis* is indeed an example of such ICT-based activities, which seek to encourage greater inclusion and mobilize the participation of diverse groups in the process of cultural production and representation. The hope is that through a dynamic, open, and collaborative digital platform, that is led by the people and managed by highly reflexive curators, the project could offer an alternative outlet for expression that is not tied to official UAE institutions or circumscribed by the their branding activities. There is always a need for alternative spaces to official institutions to develop greater nuance and metaphorical complexity beyond traditional modes of representation, and to challenge the supposed coherence/singularity of narratives presented by institutions. Digital projects and the networked affordances of Web 2.0 platforms may provide a means of breaking pre-existing institutional fences.

Web 2.0 has become, indeed, a prevalent feature of online activities in recent years. From social media to "mashupable" web-applications, digital platforms are increasingly user-driven and user-dependent. Interactions designer, Kathrin Vent, refers to Web 2.0 as "an evolutionary process of medial differentiation [which] allows multiple ways of communication across physical or cultural boundaries [enabling] already existing communication patterns to appear in a new form" (2009:135–136). In the context of curating and museum activities, the adoption and appropriation of Web 2.0 techniques and technologies often promise to enhance interactivity and engagement with cultural content, encourage user agency, and add a polysemic dimension to collections through new approaches and models of representation and archiving. Another ostensible advantage relates to the ability to transcend the limitations of physical space, enabling the creation of so-called "museums without walls" where users can generate their own material and narratives. That is not to say that all these aspects or qualities are always amenable to realization, but they too remain subject to various constraints, some of which will be reflected upon in the remainder of this article together with the advantages of a digitally mediated art platform.

Digital engagement and participation

As an art platform, *Autopoiesis* allows for a mobile aesthetic and digital forms of participation that are not attached to a particular pre-given meaning or pre-defined perspective. Instead, meaning is created through the multiplicity of users' materials themselves and audience interpretations in a bottom-up fashion. The project responds to the tension between two cultural tropes: an institutionally guided culture based on particular understandings of art and Emarati heritage, and the reality of a highly diverse culture and a large migrant population. Rather than focusing on specific events or particular moments in history, as is often the case with traditional styles of curating and exhibiting, *Autopoiesis* is more interested in the fluidity and the humble layer of the everyday (*Autopiesis* 2014) by way of presenting a more hybrid image of the UAE and allowing for different ontological perspectives. The project encourages people from all backgrounds to submit any form of art— poetry, video/audio materials, photographs, prose, paintings, drawings, etc., offering the opportunity for participation and engagement (Figure 1).

Engagement is indeed a term that is often used in discussions on museum strategies and cultural processes. Stephen Bitgood defines engagement as "deep sensory-perceptual, mental and/or affective involvement [requiring] some type of exertion or concentration as well as a sufficient amount of time to engage" (quoted in Ridge 2013). More than a quick "like" on Facebook or a retweet on Twitter, engagement demands meaningful participation and involvement (Ridge 2013). As a digital and public-driven project, *Autopoiesis* relies heavily on members of the UAE public (locals, residents, and visitors) to populate the platform with their own content as an exercise of self-creation and self-expression. Without users' content, *Autopoiesis* would be merely an empty container. The project is therefore inherently participatory and engaging in at least three fundamental ways: firstly, through its contributory character and reliance on user-generated content; secondly, in the sense that it acts as a platform for hosting contributions and giving people the freedom to choose the medium, form, and context of their contributions; and, thirdly, it is in the way the project incites people to pause and think reflexively and critically about issues of identity, culture, and belonging. By asking "What does the UAE identity, culture and life represent and mean to you?", *Autopoiesis* opens up a space for engaging with one of the most important, timely and, at times, contentious questions concerning the UAE.

How people respond to such a question is something the project has left open to contributors both in terms of format and themes. Some have responded through the medium of photography, while others have chosen drawings or videos, prose or painting. Some engaged directly with social issues such as migration, labor, climate, and unity. Others chose a more metaphorical approach through illustrations of ideas, such as, "the sand castle", "the chair", "desert", "forgotten streets", the duality of "tradition and innovation", etc. (see the artworks display on http://www.autopoiesis.io) (Figures 2 and 3). The above two artworks are examples of the diverse contributions submitted to *Autopoiesis*. Each represents a singular way of relating to the question of the UAE identity and culture. Together they reveal the eclectic nature of the UAE, creating a mosaic of images and a cacophony of voices. Importantly, as a digital platform that is open to people from different backgrounds and social strata, and to artists and amateurs alike, *Autopoiesis* aims to flatten the hierarchy often defining art and culture and dissolve the boundaries between contributors and experts. In her discussion on public memory in the digital age, Ekaterina Haskins argues that the digital space can level the traditional hierarchy between author, text, and audience by decentering authorial agency and "preventing any one agent from imposing narrative and ideological closure upon the data" (2007:406). This is the case insofar as the digital space and Web 2.0 technologies allow users to supply their own content and actively choose their own paths through the platform instead of rigidly following a museum audio-tour format, for instance. In this sense and instead of acting as mere consumers of a linear story, audiences become active participants in creating meaning and choosing how to engage with images and narratives.

Admittedly, however, the extent of *Autopoiesis'* participatory and engagement efforts have been limited by a number of factors. First, as a digital platform, *Autopoiesis* might unwittingly privilege those who are "connected", that is, those who have access to the Internet and the ability/desire to participate to an online platform. Although the UAE is one of the most Internet enabled and digitally connected countries in the Gulf and the Middle East region, access to online spaces and technologies remains unequal across social strata and along the familiar uneven socio-economic conditions of the population. Vora (2012:791–792) argues that Internet access, for individual users, depends on where one lives in the UAE: "Expatriate neighbourhoods (usually in newer apartment buildings) in city centres are more wired, meaning that many middle- and upper-class foreign residents have Internet access at home". Parenthetically and as Vora goes on to explain, although the category of "expatriate" implies the foreign population of a country, in the case of the UAE the term carries classed and raced connotations that privilege Western and white people. As for the scores of South Asian "migrants", they are often the subject of governmental as well as privatized efforts to "clean up" neighbourhoods and the cities' shopping malls (Vora 2012:790, 801) (Figures 4 and 5).

As such, expatriates tend to experience a level of inclusion, belonging and access that is not afforded to migrant workers whose socio-economic situations may inhibit their ownership of or access to communication and Internet technologies, thereby limiting their ability to participate in online and digitally mediated civic activities. After all and as Astra Taylor (2014) reminds us, the Internet often reflects real-world inequalities.

Issues of belonging and citizenship are what Al Naiar's contribution to *Autopoiesis*, *UAE Autopsy* (2014), directly focuses on. This raw and roughly edited documentary video features a series of interviews with migrant workers (mainly South Asian shopkeepers) and a local citizen, asking politically charged questions about citizenship, rights, belonging and inclusion in the context of the UAE. The documentary maker, who is a UAE-born non-citizen, seeks to address the problematic nature of citizenry issues and civic participation in the country, and include the faces and opinions of those who are largely excluded from the dominant narrative and official cultural spaces (Figure 6).[1]

Contributions to *Autopoiesis* by migrant laborers *themselves* were, nonetheless, few as the project initially faced the challenge of outreach, especially that most of its work and activities have been conducted virtually. The fact that the project curator is not physically based in the UAE and mostly reliant on virtual and online networks for publicity and outreach limits the extent to

[1.] See http://www.autopoiesis.io/submissions/1000035/.

Figure 4. Jan Lemitz (2014 [2010]): "Dubai Habitat", a series of photographs capturing the transient constellations that are the shacks and shelters next to the construction site of Jumeirah marina. "A rather informal part of the economy, their existence follows the cycles of real estate development in Dubai. These sites become oftentimes

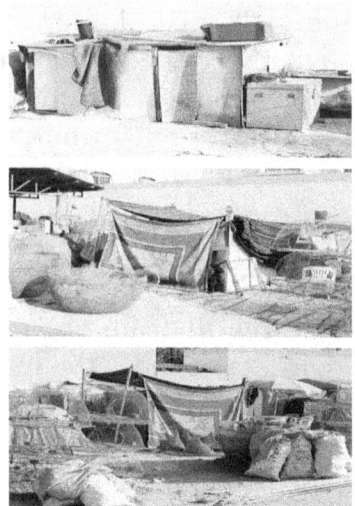

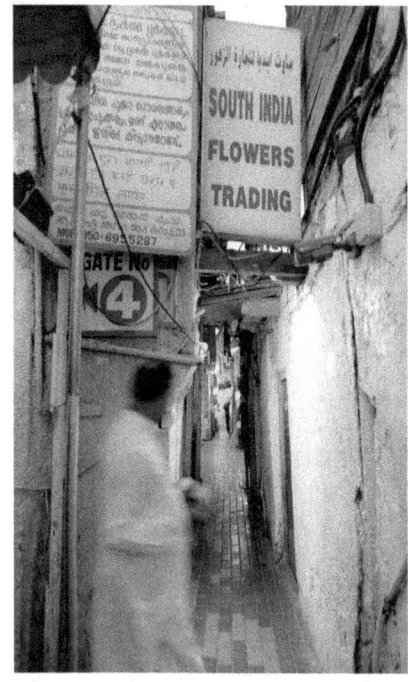

Figure 5. Reem Saeed (2014): "Mandir: Life Between Alleys" provides a glimpse of "the fading beauty of old alleys" within the Emirates. The series of photographs is "a documentation of a particular hidden tiny alley where a small Hindu Temple is situated. An aggressive, colorful contrast between the modern and the traditional."

which *Autopoiesis*, as a digital endeavor with limited funds, can reach many people on the ground and engage a greater number of unrepresented and unprivileged groups who might not necessarily have an online presence.

The project has relied largely on social media platforms, its existing networks in the UAE and on relevant cultural organizations to publicize its activities and increase its outreach. However, relying on certain networks, organizations and methods of outreach remains unavoidably linked to the problem of preferentialism and bias (see Barabasi and Albert 1999), which, while not being necessarily the intention of digital projects, is nonetheless a potential byproduct of uneven connectivity and unequal online exposure and access. For instance, artists, organizations, and networks with an already established (online) presence and cultural capital are of course the easiest to discover and reach. Focusing mainly on these carries the risk of obscuring other potential participants who might not have a digital presence or be identified as professional artists. Ultimately, this issue of unintentional preferentialism can also limit the potential of digital projects, such as *Autopoiesis*, to offer a platform for diverse voices and eclectic expressions. As such, one of the important tasks for *Autopoiesis* was to find ways to overcome the material and local limitations and reach out to individuals and groups who lack access to Internet technologies and online spaces. This task necessitated looking beyond the project's own networks and associations and recognizing the bias (even unintentional) inherent in the act of overlying on certain digital platforms and privileging those already connected. Finding collaborators *on the ground* who are able to directly access groups and communities, who would otherwise be hard to reach digitally, was key to achieving a greater level of diverse contributions and to the fulfillment (partially at least) of *Autopoiesis'* objectives.[2]

What the above reflections indicate is that any digital space or project, regardless of how global and networked it is, remains subject to similar local considerations and material constraints as is the case with physical spaces and projects. The virtual is by no means disembodied and digital media are "material objects in their own right", as Witcomb (2007) puts it. In other words, digitally enabled cultural processes and Web 2.0 platforms cannot be understood without considering the spatial settings and material realities of their contexts.

In their article on the relationship between digitization, materiality, and cultural artefacts, Peteri and her colleagues (2013) argue that the popularization of the Internet and computer technologies in general has managed to reveal "how 'virtual' practices don't exist apart from the everyday material practices". In the case of Autopoiesis, this relates to how

[2.] For instance, Autopoiesis connected with the Gulf Labor organization in the hope of soliciting submissions of artworks that address issues of migrant workers. As mentioned earlier, the organization is a coalition of activist artists and has been successful in attracting international attention to the human rights issues concerning the construction of the Saadiyat Island. It has the advantage of direct contact on the ground with workers themselves and, as such, is able to document creatively their everyday experiences. One of the primary aims of Gulf Labor (2014) is indeed to make "visible" that which has been removed from public view and from local policies. This is mainly the case of construction workers who have been instrumental to the building of the UAE and yet remained excluded from its citizenry. As such, connecting with Gulf Labor and its activist work opens up a further channel of outreach for Autopoiesis, facilitating forms of cultural participation and expression that are not reliant solely on online and digital platforms but also on physical and face-to-face communication with laborers and other relevant groups.

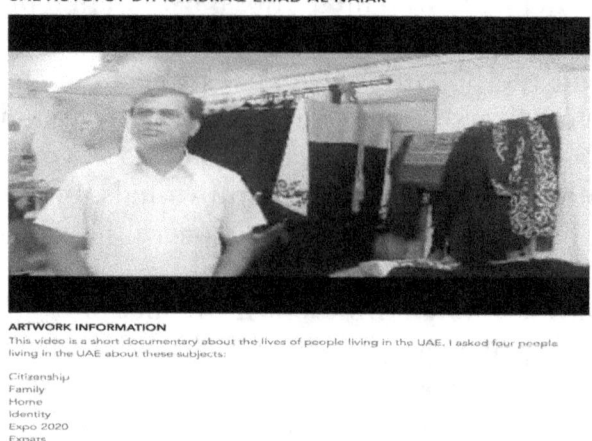

Figure 6. Istabraq Emad Al Naiar (2014): "Autopsy".

the online platform provided by the website represents a space that is still reliant on a server, a data center and physical media artifacts (computers, mobile devices, cameras, etc.) for its own functioning and its ability to be populated by content and material. This also relates, as discussed earlier, to issues regarding digital access and equity, the kind of governance systems and policies in place that either allow or restrict the material conditions under which participants are enabled (or not) to have access and contribute to the project. As such, Autopoiesis, like many other digital initiatives, is a project that is continually oscillating between the global and the local, the virtual and the physical, the digital and the material.

The Virtual Physical: Autopoiesis 2.0 exhibition

In October 2014, a related live exhibition under the name *Autopoiesis 2.0* was held as part of the Arts and Humanities Festival at King's College London. While the online exhibition space of *Autopoiesis* aimed to capture and create a multivocal environment for cultural expression, the physical space of the exhibition sought to provide the viewer with a "window" into this space through the display of artworks that have been submitted to *Autopoiesis*. Instead of exhibiting the "physical" prints or embodiments of these artworks, *Autopoiesis 2.0* carried over the notion and practice of the digital into the physical space of the exhibition by opting for the digital projection of artworks through multiple large screens, invoking a similar experience to the web-browsing environment of *Autopoiesis*. On a practical level, this enabled the display of a greater number of contributions than what would have been possible through physical prints, given the limited exhibition space. This is another instance of how the digital is able to provide more exposure to a variety of works by overcoming some of the spatial limitations. On a conceptual level, this was also intended as a playful reminder of the

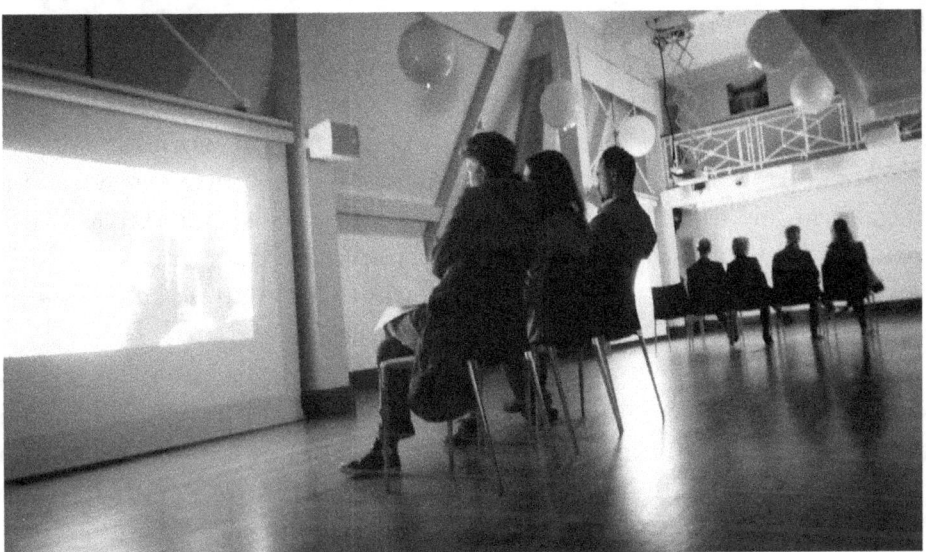

Figure 7. *Autopoiesis 2.0* exhibition.

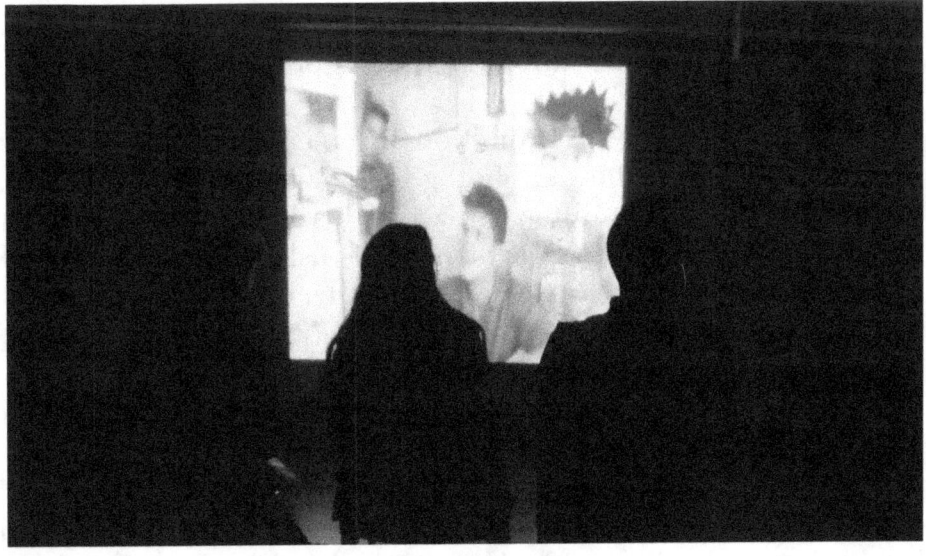

Figure 8. *Autopoiesis 2.0* exhibition.

"materiality" of the digital and an opportunity to engage with the interplays and tensions between the virtual and the physical (Figure 7).

In her review of the *Autopoiesis 2.0* exhibition, McAuliffe (2014) argued that translating the digital nature of the project into analog content (canvases, printed photographs, films on separate screens, etc.) within the exhibition space could have potentially reinstated the very territorial limitations of official UAE cultural institutions that *Autopoiesis 2.0* attempted to challenge. McAuliffe goes on to suggest that in showcasing artworks by a variety of UAE residents and visitors through the open topology of digital networks, "*Autopoiesis 2.0* offers counternarratives not only to the dominant cultural narrative supported by UAE institutions, but also to the very conceptual and spatial framework through which they offer these narratives" (ibid.). The digital has thus allowed *Autopoiesis* to reimagine the cultural space and heritage of the UAE and provide a more inclusive platform for its multi-ethnic and multi-national contemporary population.

The exhibition used both audio and visual elements (photographic and film material) to create an immersive ambiance, which stimulated free thinking and interpretation, and incited visitors' assimilation into the cultural milieu of the UAE as represented by the exhibited material. This was further encouraged by the minimal information provided to visitors about the various artworks. Apart from supplying an informative leaflet about the contributions featured in the exhibition, visitors were left to freely bring their own interpretations, meanings, and narratives to these artworks reinforcing the "autopoetic" nature of the exhibition and the project as a whole.

The spatial arrangement of the exhibition space consisted of two screens that faced each other and showed photographic artworks in the format of slide-shows, which moved at different paces. This intended to provide the viewer with the possibility to interact simultaneously with images linked to distinct themes and narratives. A third screen, facing the entrance to the exhibition, was used to project the film contributions (Figure 8).

The various sounds emanating from these films created an ambient background noise, puncturing the stillness and blank interior of the exhibition space. The interactions between image and sound offered a unique audio-visual environment while maintaining an empty space, which evoked at once a sense of place (the UAE) as well as placeless-ness through the cacophony of sounds and mosaic of images. As succinctly described by McAuliffe (2014), "[p]rojecting films not only deterritorialized the artwork from any single UAE institution or locality, but also deterritorialized the physical space in which the art was seemingly reterritorialized: the exhibition room". This deterritorialization is indeed what enables the exploration of more creative and nomadic responses based on digital and networked Web 2.0 topologies and affordances as opposed to the spatially restrictive and somewhat sedentary arrangements of dominant cultural institutions (for instance, cultural artifacts housed in official exhibition spaces and discrete archives). Moreover, through its spatial arrangement and by projecting artworks on various screens, *Autopoiesis 2.0* created, at once, a degree of spatial fluidity and free movement as well as a sense of territorial awareness among visitors. McAuliffe (2014) described the spatial experience of the exhibition in the following way:

> Visitors exhibited a hyper-awareness of the space they, and others, took up — perhaps more attuned to the territory they occupy with the absence of any material elements or masses of people automatically enforcing boundaries at the exhibition. This behavior revealed the way in which visitors explored the space relationally rather than through externally carved-out, designated areas — and reflected the way in which, lacking enforced institutional boundaries, a collection of various individuals can relationally explore, shape, and legitimize a cultural space.

In addition to this spatial dimension of the project, the "temporal" aspect is also another important dimension that often plays out in the discussions regarding issues of sustainability and preservation vis-à-vis digital art projects in general. Given the transitory nature of temporary exhibitions and the virtual aspect of web-enabled art platforms, it is often argued that this type of art project inevitably contains an element of ephemerality that contrasts with the more permanent nature of physical museums and collections. There is to be sure a general uneasiness over the issue of ephemerality in relation to digital art platforms, which often, as pointed out by Marvin Lin (2015), manifests in anxieties about the future of these platforms and what might become of their content. The challenge of constantly changing technologies and software together with the persisting bias toward physical artifacts within the traditional curatorial imaginary have contributed to such anxieties and sense of unease. In a way, the temporal argument around the supposed ephemerality of digital platforms is also based in the spatial argument around the supposed immateriality of these platforms. As Kaminska (2009:43) postulates, "[i]mmateriality is primarily a question of space, and ephemerality one of time [...]. Ephemerality is often suggested as a consequence of the immaterial nature of software". But as discussed earlier, the digital is by no means immaterial, be it in terms of technicality or in terms of context. And even the most material of objects is still bound to degenerate eventually. Correlatively and from an audience's perspective, Lin (2015) suggests that "art has never been a solely tangible experience anyway; we're not meant to 'touch' paintings in order to experience them, and any materials used to create so-called tangible art won't last forever— thus, making all art inherently time-based." Temporariness is therefore an inevitable feature of artworks.

As such, rather than judging the future sustainability, and by extension the "legitimacy", of digital art projects against that of physical museums and analog collections, one needs to rethink the idea and practice of preservation itself in light of the dynamic materiality and fluid temporality of digital objects and platforms. For this, new modes of conservation and different strategies of documentation and preservation need to be explored and encouraged in order to tap into and harness the potential of interactivity, adaptability, performativity, and reproducibility that are characteristic of the digital ecosystem. In their interview on the use of new media for the collection and preservation of digital art, Rinehart and Ippolito (2014) argue that:

> We should be looking at paradigms that are more contingent than static [...]. Casting a wider net can help preservationists jettison our culture's implicit metaphor of stony durability in favor of one of fluid adaptability [...] Digital preservationists can learn from media that thrive by reinterpretation and reuse [...] Change will happen. Don't resist it; use it, guide it. Let art breathe; it will tell you what it needs.

In a concrete sense, a new media-driven paradigm of art preservation would entail a number of strategies and steps that are at once technical as well as conceptual, and which need to be integrated into the overall plan of digital collection management. These include keeping abreast with the technological developments in new media forms and digital infrastructures in order to establish the optimal ways of storing and displaying digital material, and overcoming potential incompatibility of software; periodic migration of materials onto new formats or platforms to ensure continuous functionality; regular system maintenance and backups; sustaining the interactive features of Web 2.0-based platforms; and, on a more epistemological level, re-evaluating and challenging traditional perceptions around the value and meaning of digital art, and even embracing the ephemeral qualities of some forms of art rather than seeing them as delegitimizing factors. The point is that, just as physical art objects need a level of care and conservation, so too do digital materials. This, however, does not mean that digital or virtual art projects need to emulate the traditional preservation strategies of physical museums nor should every cultural or art initiative and output be subjected to permanent archiving. It might be that it is museums themselves that need to learn from the fluidity, adaptability, openness, and experimental nature of digital projects and their preservation approaches. This need not be a question of hierarchy or competition, but that of lesson learning, collaboration, and cross-pollination of strategies.

In terms of *Autopoiesis*, the project's preservation strategy is primarily around ensuring a long term support for web hosting and server management for the project's website, as it is the main platform for receiving, hosting, and exhibiting public art submissions. A periodic backup process is conducted for all material residing on *Autopoiesis* platform. As the project keeps growing, the project curator will continue to collaborate with the platform designers to explore optimal approaches for the project's sustainability.

Conclusion: Toward an autopoietic public art 2.0

Issues of participation, engagement, and access remain important concerns in processes of cultural production, curation, representation, and dissemination. This article examined the curatorial role of Web 2.0 platforms, especially in enabling forms of participatory culture beyond the frameworks and criteria of dominant institutions and their traditional curatorial practices. This examination has led to the conclusion that while digital platforms herald a potential for greater public participation in culture and the possibility of wider and more democratized forms of access and inclusion, they also remain subject to some familiar limitations and inextricably tied to local constraints and material contexts. The example of *Autopoiesis* is a case in point. By reflecting on the aims, advantages, and limitations of this Web 2.0-mediated public art project, we were able to unravel the complex socio-political and practical issues which directly and indirectly affect the functioning, outreach, and success of the project.

Currently, the majority of mainstream UAE cultural institutions are mainly preoccupied with investing in the building of grand eye-catching projects such as the new Cultural District of the Saadiyat Island, which will be home to some of the most ambitious and extravagant museum projects in the region, including the Louvre Abu Dhabi and Guggenheim Abu Dhabi. Underlying these projects is the desire to gain instant recognition and prestige on the international stage of arts and culture by heavily investing in branding activities in the form of a rather costly association with already established Western cultural brands (e.g. Louvre) and the commissioning of celebrity architects to design these colossal "signature" museum buildings (e.g. Norman Foster, Frank Gehry, Zaha Hadid, and Jean Nouvel) (see McClellan 2012). While these cultural branding activities help "spectacularize" the urban environment of the Emirates and promote the country as a progressive and civilised place, as Ponzini (2011:258) argues, they also risk obscuring the more diverse cultural forms and expressions of the ethnically varied groups that represent the region. Finding ways to account for, represent, and communicate this diversity and multiplicity of cultures and identities is a necessary curatorial task. One of the aims of *Autopoiesis*, as a curatorial project, was indeed to contribute to this process by stimulating further engagement with the wider socio-political and cultural issues and contexts surrounding artistic production and dissemination in the UAE and beyond.

At the same time and in constituting an experimental exploration into the curatorial potential of Web 2.0, *Autopoiesis* has been able to critically shed some light on the value and limitations of a user-centred and digitally mediated curatorial practice, including the conceptual and practical tensions between the virtual and the physical dimensions of Web 2.0 which, as mentioned earlier, prompt the need to consider the wider local realities and material contexts of digital projects and their platforms instead of regarding them in a purely technological sense. Overall, what *Autopoiesis* raises as an overarching question is also the changing role of curator in light of the advent of digital communication environments and the exigencies of a globalized, postcolonial, and networked world, whereby curating is no longer merely about the behind-the-scenes activities of collating artworks and finding a meaningful thread to bind them, but also about actively facilitating and motivating audience/user engagement, input and collaboration through various means, including Web 2.0. It is therefore crucial to continue to observe, analyze, and empirically explore this growing interplay between the practices of curating and the technologies of Web 2.0, especially in terms of how, and the extent to which, their combination can critically contribute to a more inclusive and ethical representation of the diversity and hybridity of contemporary societies within processes of cultural production, mediation, and exhibition.

Author's Acknowledgements: *I wish to thank the Cultural Institute at King's College London for supporting* Autopoiesis *project. Thanks also to Kerry McAuliffe and Oana Mihut for their valuable help with the project, and to Tzara Talissa Makdessi, Ossman Saeb Salam, and Shan Huang for assistance with outreach activities.*

References

Al Falasi, Hamad. (2014) Desert Bejewelled. <http://www.autopoiesis.io/submissions/1000040/> (Accessed September 2014).

Al Naiar, Istabraq. (2014) UAE Autopsy. <http://www.autopoiesis.io/submissions/1000035/> (Accessed September 2014).

Ajana, Btihaj. (2015) Branding, Legitimation and the Power of Museums: The Case of the Louvre Abu Dhabi. *Museum and Society* 13 (3): 316–335.

Autopoiesis. (2014) Autopoiesis Art Project. <http://www.autopoiesis.io> (Accessed 6 January 2014).

Barabasi, Albert-László, and Réka Albert. (1999) Emergence of Scaling in Random Networks. Science 286 (5439): 509–512.

Batty, David. (2012) The Rise of the Gulf Art Scene. <http://www.theguardian.com/artanddesign/2012/apr/16/rise-of-gulf-art-scene> (Accessed 4 November 2013).

Batty, David. (2013) Conditions for Abu Dhabi's migrant workers 'shame the west'. <https://www.theguardian.com/world/2013/dec/22/abu-dhabi-migrant-workers-conditions-shame-west> (Accessed January 2014).

Blake, Sean. (2014) The Untitled Chair Project. <http://www.autopoiesis.io/submissions/1000023/> (Accessed September 2014).

Bourdieu, Pierre. (1968 [1984]) The Field of Cultural Production: Essays on Art and Literature. <http://web.mit.edu/allanmc/www/bourdieu3.pdf> (Accessed 28 October 2012).

Cabiddu, Francesca, et al. (2014) Social Media Affordances: Enabling Customer Engagement. Annals of Tourism Research 48: 175–192.

Cairns, Susan, and Danny Birchall. (2013) Curating the Digital World: Past Preconceptions, Present Problems, Possible Futures. <http://mw2013.museumsandtheweb.com/paper/curating-the-digital-world-past-preconceptions-present-problems-possible-futures/> (Accessed 20 February 2014).

Davidson, Christopher. (2013) Abu Dhabi's New Economy: Oil, Investment and Development. <http://www.mepc.org/journal/middle-east-policy-archives/abu-dhabis-new-economy-oil-investment-and-domestic-development> (Accessed 28 January 2014).

Gulf Labor. (2014) Observations and Recommendations after Visiting Saadiyat Island and Related Sites. <http://gulflabor.org/wp-content/uploads/2014/04/gl_REPORT_APR30.pdf> (Accessed 3 January 2015).

Gulf Labor. (n.d.) <https://www.facebook.com/gulflaborgroup> (Accessed 26 February 2014).
Haskins, Ekaterina. (2007) Between Archive and Participation: Public Memory in a Digital Age. Rhetoric Society Quarterly 37 (4): 401–422.

Kaminska, Aleksandra. (2009) Locating the Ephemeral: Capturing the Fleeting Moment in Digital Arts. *International Journal of Arts and Technology* 2 (2): 40–50.

Krysa, Joasia. (2006) Curating Immateriality: The Work of the Curator in the Age of Network Systems. <https://trac.v2.nl/export/7535/rui/.../Curating%20immateriality.pdf> (Accessed 28 October 2013).

Lemitz, Jan. (2014 [2010]) DXB: Dubai Habitat. <http://www.autopoiesis.io/submissions/1000054/> (Accessed September 2014).

Lichty, Patrick. (2003) Reconfiguring the Museum Electronic Media and Emergent Curatorial Models. <http://www.intelligentagent.com/archive/vo3%5B1%5D.01.curation.lichty.PDF> (Accessed 28 January 2014).

Lin, Marvin. (2015) Widening the Scope: On Intangibility, Embodiment and Ephemerality. <http://blogs.walkerart.org/design/2015/06/15/widening-the-scope-on-intangibility-embodiment-and-ephemerality> (Accessed 9 January 2016).

Martinon, Jean-Paul. (Ed.) (2013) *The Curatorial: A Philosophy of Curating.* London: Bloomsbury.

McAuliffe, Kerry. (2014) Review of Autopoiesis 2.0 Exhibition (18–24 October 2014). <http://www.autopoiesis.io/articles/2/> (Accessed 2 January 2015).

McClellan, Andrew. (2012) Museum Expansion in the Twenty-First Century: Abu Dhabi. *Journal of Curatorial Studies* 1 (3): 271–293.

New York Times. (2015) NYU Professor is Barred by United Arab Emirates. 16 March. <http://www.nytimes.com/2015/03/17/nyregion/nyu-professor-is-barred-from-the-united-arab-emirates.html?_r=2> (Accessed 17 March 2015).

O'Reilly, Tim. (2005) What Is Web 2.0?. O'Reilly Network. <http://www.oreillynet.com/pub/a/oreilly/tim/news/2005/09/30/what-is-web-20.html/> (Accessed 4 November 2014).

Peteri, Virve, et al. (2013) Materiality of Digital Environments. <http://widerscreen.fi/numerot/2013-1/materiality-of-digital-environments/> (Accessed 4 November 2014).

Ponzini, Davide. (2011) Large Scale Development Projects and Star Architecture in the Absence of Democratic Politics: The Case of Abu Dhabi, UAE. Cities 28: 251–291.

Ridge, Mia. (2013) Digital Participation, Engagement and Crowdsourcing in Museums. <http://www.londonmuseumsgroup.org/2013/08/15/digital-participation-engagement-and-crowdsourcing-in-museums/> (Accessed 4 November 2014).

Rinehart, Richard, and Jon Ippolito. (2014) Collecting and Preserving Digital Art. <https://blogs.loc.gov/digitalpreservation/2014/11/collecting-and-preserving-digital-art-interview-with-richard-rinehart-and-jon-ippolito/> (Accessed 9 January 2016).

Saeed, Reem. (2014) Mandir: Life Between Alleys. < http://www.autopoiesis.io/submissions/1000049/> (Accessed September 2014).

Sample, Mark. (2010) The Archive or the Trace: Cultural Permanence and the Fugitive Text. <http://www.samplereality.com/2010/01/18/the-archive-or-the-trace-cultural-permanence-and-the-fugitive-text/> (Accessed 9 January 2016).

Shahani, Lavina, et al. (2008) Museums Curating Online Content Using Web 2.0: Making Cultural Production More Democratic?. <http://network.icom.museum/fileadmin/user_upload/minisites/cidoc/ConferencePapers/2008/40_papers.pdf> (Accessed 4 November 2014).

Srinivasan, Ramesh, et al. (2008) Digital Museums and Diverse Cultural Knowledge: Moving Past the Traditional Catalog. <http://rameshsrinivasan.org/wordpress/wp-content/uploads/2010/04/1-SrinivasanetalTISBlobgects.pdf> (Accessed 8 May 2014).

Taylor, Astra (2014) *The People's Platform: Taking Back Power and Culture in the Digital Age*. London: Fourth Estate.

Vent, Kathrin. (2009) Web 2.0 as an Autopoietic System: Implications for Innovative Web-Interfaces. <http://subs.emis.de/LNI/Proceedings/Proceedings148/125.pdf> (Accessed 4 November 2014).

Vora, Neha. (2012) Free Speech and Civil Discourse: Producing Expats, Locals and Migrants in the UAE English-Language Blogosphere. *Journal of the Royal Anthropological Institute* 18 (4): 787–807.

Vora, Neha. (2013) *Impossible Citizens: Dubai's Indian Diaspora*. Durham, NC: Duke University Press.

Witcomb, Andrea. (2007) The Materiality of Virtual Technologies: A New Approach to Thinking about the Impact of Multimedia in Museums. <http://mitpress.universitypressscholarship.com/view/10.7551/mitpress/9780262033534.001.0001/upso-9780262033534-chapter-3> (Accessed 4 November 2014).

The Cultural Implications of Performance

Christine Adams

Christine Adams has taught at St. Mary's College in Maryland since the fall of 1992. She has published primarily in French family and gender history, including two books: A Taste for Comfort and Status: A Bourgeois Family in Eighteenth-Century France *and* Poverty, Charity and Motherhood: Maternal Societies in Nineteenth-Century France.

Instagram, Snapchat, and YouTube have created a world that effaces the line between real life and performed reality. Academics refer to a particular type of performance as performativity: on social media, we share photos and posts that not only reflect who we are but that also construct the identity we wish to communicate. Performativity is heavily gendered, and the stakes for young women are both different and perhaps higher than for their male peers. Today, in a world dominated by social media, young women in particular seek empowerment through performing for both their friends and a wider world that often treats them as little more than sexual objects (Note 1). Some are celebrities, some are wannabe celebrities; some are simply looking for the gratification of public approval for their self-presentation while others have broader aims. We all act in a specific historical, political, and now technological context, which affects the nature of the image we try to present of ourselves as well as how it is received. This impulse to perform (and to judge those performances) is nothing new (Note 2), but conditions of and incentives for those performances are historically specific and help us understand the spectacle of social life and the consequences for the individuals who are part of the show.

And yet, despite the fact that we recognize the omnipresence of performance in our own self-presentation as well as that of others, we also claim to value transparency, sincerity, and authenticity—on TV shows such as "The Bachelor" and "The Bachelorette" in the United States, the participants always profess to be searching for that ever-elusive "sincerity" in a potential partner. In the 2016 political campaign season, one of the biggest criticisms of Hillary Clinton was her lack of authenticity. In fact, political pundits regularly suggest ways in which she could more effectively "perform authenticity," which seems like an oxymoron. In fact, it appears that Clinton's awkward wonkishness was indeed authentic. When she tried to perform the emotions that audiences clamored for, it came across as inauthentic. Celebrities, who act for a living, are better at performing those "authentic" emotions than Clinton was; not surprisingly, the most successful politicians today are often those who can enact "authenticity."

Because celebrities can effectively display emotional authenticity in support of a cause, many young women in the public eye today have entered that liminal space between culture and politics. Celebrities of all sorts frequently use their visibility toward political ends; it can be quite explicit, as in the case of Emma Watson speaking in support of feminism at the United Nations or Beyoncé using her musical performances to draw attention to fraught racial and gender issues. However, it is not only famous women who put themselves on display with a political goal in mind. SlutWalk is another kind of performance with an unambiguous political message. But for women, the simple decision to put oneself in the public sphere, to perform, and to claim a public voice can be a political act. Cultural critics have recognized the political intent in these assertions of female agency, even if, as Andi Zeisler suggests that "celebrity feminists (and the media that flocks to them) seem more comfortable with feminism as an identity than with its substance" (Zeisler 2016). Sometimes the substance of the political statement is subsumed to the spectacle of the performance.

Today in the Western world, we are used to women, famous or not, who put themselves on display. While the self-promotion of social media denizens and other celebrities is hardly universally celebrated, few see the choice to do so as dangerous, despite the real and sometimes genuinely menacing presence of misogynistic trolls who threaten outspoken women on the Internet. But the danger is far more acute in conservative settings where performance and self-display are considered not only explicitly political but also highly threatening. In a recent notorious and chilling case, Pakistani social media celebrity Qandeel Baloch's brother murdered her in an "honor killing"; he believed that her provocative videos, posted on line, brought disgrace to her family. In a country that denies fundamental rights, such as education, to many women, and enforces sexual modesty through violence, Qandeel's life and death had enormous political resonance. According to BBC news, "...The fact that many of Qandeel's videos went viral suggests a titillating fascination with confident female sexuality - along with fear of its power and of her assertion of independence" (BBC 2016). While these fears may be more intense and dangerous in traditional cultures, they exist in the Western world as well.

As a historian, when I want to better understand modern phenomena, I turn to the past. These links between celebrity, performance, and politics may seem modern and specific to our age of social media, but they have a history. As a scholar of gender in early modern France, I frequently find echoes of the present in my research. Our fascination with celebrity spectacle and the performance of gender as well as concerns about authenticity, politics, and female empowerment through sexual assertiveness are nothing new. Through the examination of moments in the past when the public obsessed about performance, authenticity, and fears of female power and sexuality, we can better understand the forces of the present that create a similar moment.

In early modern France, the members of the French royal court, especially the royal family, performed under the gaze of other courtiers, and perceived their daily lives as unfolding on a kind of stage. Contemporary writers often spoke of "the theater of the court," and considered the court of Louis XIV, the Sun King (1643–1715), the most theatrical of them all. In this context, women—for example, royal mistresses—could often exercise political influence through social networks and the performance of beauty and power. But with the onset of the Age of Enlightenment in the eighteenth century came a new insistence on the authentic and the natural. The French, under the influence of philosophes such as Jean-Jacques Rousseau, called for greater transparency in government as well as sincerity in interpersonal relations, and rejected the artificiality that had been an accepted element of court life. The elaborate dress and cosmetics of courtiers symbolized the affectations of aristocrats. The Rousseau-reading public rejected the appearance of artifice and touted instead the beauty of the simple and the "natural" in appearance and modes of interactions, especially for women— although of course, this was as much of a performance as the "artificiality" of earlier times.

As Revolution broke out in 1789, and especially during the Reign of Terror (1793–1794), restrictions on female behavior intensified; now, women were expected to act as modest *citoyennes*, open and honest, devoted to their families and supportive of democratic change, unadorned and dressed simply in white. Writers accused women who wore cosmetics and elaborate clothing that masked their true appearance of dissimulation as well as secret royalist sympathies, and exhorted them to leave behind the artifice of make-up and expensive attire. Women who could not perform Republican femininity successfully might face the guillotine.

As the puritanical political regime that stoked the Reign of Terror came to an end in the summer of 1794, during the Revolutionary month of Thermidor, women sought to reclaim a voice and assert their power and individuality in the newly relaxed atmosphere through a new kind of performance. According to François Gendron, "In reaction to republican austerity and the suffocating dictatorship of virtue, Paris was shaken by an explosion of indulgence and frivolity. With the end of the Reign of Terror came roars of laughter, a riotous race for pleasure, and a lust for life" Gendron (1993). Historians have traditionally described French society post-Thermidor and under the new government of the Directory (1795–1799) as hedonistic, in large part because of the activities of newly assertive young women in the public view who rejected the previous strictures on their dress and behavior.

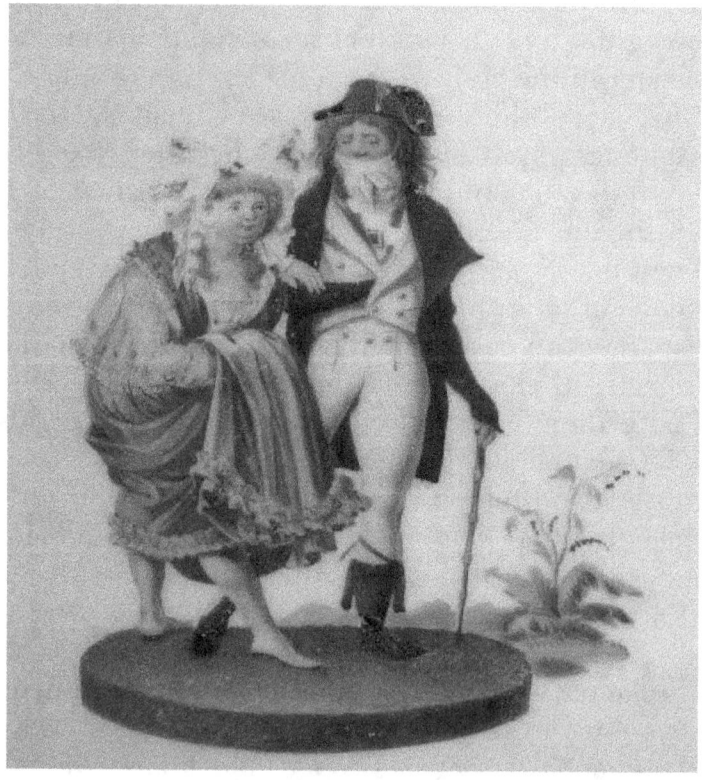

Artistic Depiction of 'Incroyables and Merveilleuses'.
By eigenes Foto (Privatsammlung) [Copyrighted free use], via Wikimedia Commons

These young women who emerged on the social and political scene were known as the *Merveilleuses*—the Marvelous Ones—and took society by storm under the Directory (Note 3). They performed beauty in a highly theatrical fashion, similar to modern-day celebrities. The historical moment was ripe for these women to make their mark; according to Caroline Rossiter, "There seems to be an obsession with visibility and the idea of seeing and being seen in the public space" under the Directory, much as there is today (Rossiter 2009:57). Fashionable and somewhat scandalous clothing played an important and explicitly political role as women rejected the modesty of the previous few years and put their bodies on display in a way that shocked contemporary observers. Most popular was the *"robe à l'athénienne"*, a light, high-waisted, Greek costume, made of muslin or gauze, "which was white and practically transparent. Greek-style sandals, and rings on the toes were fashionable accessories for such an outfit" (Lyons 1975:143). Observers were most fascinated by the see-through effect of the new clothes, highly flattering to those with an attractive figure. Many criticized the sexually provocative dress of these women, but the *Merveilleuses* and the *Incroyables* (the Incredible Ones, their male counterparts) created a new mood of glamour as people crowded around to watch these new celebrities attend theater performances or gather at the Tivoli Gardens. The public and the burgeoning press examined their activities and appearance with fascination, as did politicians, many of whom resented their defiant flair that seemed to reject the serious business of republicanism.

Like the celebrities who perform for us today—the Kardashians come to mind—these women were beautiful, glamorous, fashionable, and omnipresent. Basking in their wealth, beauty, style, a riveted media and a fascinated public, the *Merveilleuses* drew attention from both the political class and a popular audience (Note 4). Their frequent appearances at the Frascati gambling house and gardens, as well as Tivoli and Longchamps, were recorded in the press, and crowds waited to see them arrive at these venues. One imagines a red carpet in the breathless descriptions recorded in a wide variety of new journals that played the role of our modern paparazzi and social media platforms, commenting regularly on the fashions and activities of these women.

Women associated with the *Merveilleuses*, such as Thérésia Tallien—described by Elizabeth Amann as "queen of the merveilleuses, the arbiter of chic and the cynosure of Directory society" (Amman 2015:50) —and her companions such as Joséphine de Beauharnais (future wife of Napoleon), Madame de

Château-Regnault, Fortunée Hamelin, Aimée de Coigny, and *salonnière* Juliette de Récamier—became shorthand for the period as a whole. To make reference once again to the Kardashians, they sometimes seemed famous simply for being famous. But there was also a political intent in the carefully honed performances of the *Merveilleuses*, who were, in some cases, suspected of royalist sympathies. Aileen Ribeiro has argued that the revealing outfits that fashionable women wore in the years following the Reign of Terror "were a direct mockery of established morality and the almost bourgeois virtues advocated by Robespierre during the Terror" (Ribeiro 1986:117). Further, the choice of these women to showcase cosmetics, expensive clothing, and other luxurious items was also a political statement, seconding the efforts of the French political elite to revive the national economy and lighten the political mood at a time of war and deprivation (Note 5). They promoted the conspicuous consumption that undergirds a capitalist society, and the display of their almost naked bodies in their transparent dresses was a new kind of "authenticity." Fervent Jacobins, who resented the frivolity and overt sexuality that replaced earlier Revolutionary mores, fulminated against Madame Tallien's "illegitimate" control over public opinion in late 1794, (Note 6) and the *Merveilleuses* played an important role in the salons that continued to proliferate under the Directory. Until Napoleon Bonaparte came to power in 1799 and limited the social and political influence of women, the *Merveilleuses* occupied an important political and cultural position.

To come back to the issues of performance, display and authenticity, I began this essay by suggesting that this notion of life as performance is nothing new; William Shakespeare famously wrote "All the world's a stage," even before French courtiers wrote about the "theater of the court." Although most individuals are conscious that they perform for others, they tend to behave in ways that social pressures dictate. It is when an individual's performance is new or challenges those norms that we take notice; when Qandeel Baloch asserted her right to perform sexuality, Pakistanis and the world were riveted. For the individual, a transgressive performance may be more "authentic" than adherence to social norms, and is often empowering and politically resonant. But "empowering and politically resonant," especially in the hands of women, can be threatening, especially at particular historical moments. Revolutionary France was a particularly fraught historical moment, and it's not surprisingly that the new and visible role that women asserted for themselves under the Directory created a backlash in some circles. More generally, the efforts of the *Merveilleuses* to draw attention to themselves and to insert themselves into the cultural and political arena undercut the clear gender boundaries that male revolutionaries had tried to draw at the very moment the French were engaged in a heated debate about the role of both women and men in the new political system. Revolutionary politicians argued that their skillful deployment of beauty and fashion might distract men from the important work of politics, and allow women to insert themselves into the debate. It is not surprising that Napoleon eventually took steps to limit the influence of women. Against a highly politicized backdrop, all public—and even private—actions have political resonance.

The same is true today. Young women have more opportunities than ever to put themselves on display and to use their physical presence to shape political and social discourse in ways that can make the guardians of tradition unhappy. Performance itself, whether authentic-seeming or highly stylized, is a political and often empowering act for women—and certainly, it can challenge gender boundaries in a way that makes many uncomfortable at a time when those boundaries are under attack as never before. Qandeel Baloch probably recognized this, but continued to assert her right to be seen and heard. It can be dangerous to claim the right to perform, to occupy space, to influence public discourse, and to show a more "authentic" self than others are ready to accept.

Notes

1. For a review of two recent books on this topic, see Zoë Heller (2016).
2. William Egginton (2003) argues that the culture of spectacle that emerged with the Renaissance court and theater dramatically changed our experience of the space we inhabit and created a world in which space became theatrical. In this world, individuals became performers for a larger public.
3. I examine some of the issues discussed below in Adams (2014)
4. Gendron particularly emphasizes the influence of these individuals in the post-Thermidor era in The Gilded Youth of Thermidor.
5. (Spang 2002:110–25) suggests that the efforts of the social elite to seek pleasure and luxury was at least in part an effort to restore the economy and to soothe political anxieties following the tensions of the Reign of Terror and at a time when the French economy was still experiencing the effects of war.
6. See for example, the Journal de Paris, no. 102, 12 Nivose Year III (January 1, 1795), 412.

References

Adams, Christine. (2014) 'Venus of the Capitol': Madame Tallien and the Politics of Beauty under the Directory. *French Historical Studies* 37 (4): 599–629.

Amman, Elizabeth. (2015) *Dandyism in the Age of Revolution: The Art of the Cut.* Chicago and London: University of Chicago Press.

BBC News. (2016) "Qandeel Baloch, Social Media Celebrity 'killed by brother'," *BBC News*, July 16. http://www.bbc.com/news/world-asia-36814258.

Egginton, William. (2003) *How the World Became a Stage: Presence, Theatricality, and the Question of Modernity.* Albany: State University of New York.

Gendron, François. (1993) *The Gilded Youth of Thermidor.* trans. James Cookson. Montreal and Kingston: McGill-Queen's University Press.

Heller, Zoë. (2016) 'Hot' Sex & Young Girls. *The New York Review of Books*, August 18. <http://www.nybooks.com/articles/2016/08/18/hot-sex-young-girls/>

Lyons, Martyn. (1975) *France under the Directory.* Cambridge: Cambridge University Press.

Ribeiro, Aileen. (1986) *Dress and Morality.* Oxford and New York: Berg.

Rossiter, Caroline. (2009) Early French Caricature (1795–1830) and English Influence. *European Comic Art* 9: 57.

Spang, Rebecca L. (2002) The Frivolous French: 'Liberty of Pleasure' and the End of Luxury. In *Taking Liberties: Problems of a New Order from the French Revolution to Napoleon*, eds. H.G. Brown and J.A. Miller. Manchester: Manchester University Press.

Zeisler, Andi. (2016) Has Celebrity Feminism Failed? *The Guardian*, May 16. <https://www.theguardian.com/lifeandstyle/2016/may/16/has-celebrity-feminism-failed>

Cultural Stratification and Cultural Policies: Perspectives of Cultural Globalism, The Case of Croatia

Nada Švob-Đokić

Dr. Nada Švob-Đokić is a Senior Researcher Emeritus in the Culture and Communication Department at the Institute for Development and International Relations (IRMO), Zagreb. Her main research interests include cultural and media transitions and public policies in these areas, cultural globalization, and cultural identity studies.

Abstract

In this article, the processes of cultural stratification are explored as related to the context of globalism. The globalized cultural context enables fast and effective exchange of content, values, symbols, and meanings within the newly created cultural spaces (in Southeast Europe) and thus influences cultural change reflected in the processes of cultural stratification within national cultures. Although the stratification processes are not always fully transparent, standardized, or clearly visible, certain types of culture can be distinguished and these are described here as *institutional culture, independent culture*, and *market-oriented culture*. Functional links among these cultural types have not always been entirely established, but they nevertheless lead to different approaches to cultural policy making. An illustration of such situation is put forward by the presentation of the Croatian case. The roles and potential functioning of cultural policies are explored in this respect. It is observed that cultural policies tend to decentralize and diversify; they tend to encompass an increased cultural production and cultural exchange, but their functional responses to global influences and the issuing cultural stratification are weak and often inconsistent.

Introduction

The recent cultural transitions in post-socialist Southeast European countries have opened a number of issues related to cultural change and in particular to cultural stratification inspired by or directly linked to cultural globalization processes. As diversified cultural practices have occurred during the last about twenty-odd years, the previously more or less standardized cultural policies (reflecting the concept of welfare state and profuse investment in development of cultural institutions) have been changed to stress more liberal tendencies in overall social development of all post-socialist countries. The Southeast European cultural space has become ever more diversified and ever more tolerant of different local cultural traditions as well as of global influences affecting them. At the same time, national cultural identification and building up of cultural identity has become a strongly expressed cultural issue on national and local levels. The reference point to such developments is cultural change prompted by globalism and often sustained by cultural strategies and policies.

The overall approach to the analysis of global impacts on local cultures presumes that the systemic transition has initiated a restructuring and reorganization of cultural activities and cultural values, as well as the (re-) establishment of more or less consistent cultural policies open to global (i.e., European) influences. This has supported changes of local cultures and encouraged local responses to global impacts.

In this respect, a general view of globalization and globalism is here presented to mark the inception of new cultural spaces and the raising awareness of stratification processes affecting Southeast European cultures. A general overview of the role and performance of local cultural policies (seen through their impact on the ongoing cultural restructuration) may help elucidate the national and local efforts invested to follow global trends and influences.

The case of Croatia illustrates well such processes. It shows that the notion of national culture is getting closer to the concept of a specific cultural space (e.g., European or regional Southeast European) through the diversification and decentralization of cultural policies, and that the issue of national identification has evolved to promote a variety of different aims and practices. In this respect, the Croatian case is useful for the study of cultural change in Southeast Europe. It is, however, limited by its specificity and concentration on the internalized cultural values and practices.

The study of some similar developments and cultural practices incited by global influences that can be traced in other Southeast European countries indicates that dissimilarities among Southeast European cultures are growing. They may appear disguised as "specificities" of national cultural traditions which strongly support the preservation of national cultural frameworks. Global influences and their impacts do not therefore provide for a kind of regional Southeast European or even European cultural identification.

The strongest and most visible global influences are technological and communicational. As culture is "the source of *newness*" and thus "drives" technology (Hartley, Wen, and Siling Li 2015:14) the global technological influences do not only affect cultural creativity, but they are also reflected in all types of cultural stratification. It is visible in countries such as Romania, Bosnia, Serbia, Macedonia, or Bulgaria where cultural stratification is, as well as in Croatia, influenced by the development of vivacious NGO sectors that strongly support cultural production, particularly the types "abandoned" by the state.

The public impact of the emerging civil society on cultural production and change in *Romania* has become "more pragmatic and specifically targeted to the needs of cultural life" as it influenced the provision of "an articulated framework for grants," incited local pilot projects of public interest and raised public awareness and transparency of management of culture (Balsan 2012).

New actors such as foundations or private cultural institutions, organized by NGOs, have emerged on the *Bulgarian* cultural scene (Andreeva and Tomova 2011). Civil society has considerably influenced the formulation of a "new cultural policy model" that brought decentralization of cultural policy and included minority cultures participation in the national cultural activities.

Serbia, Macedonia, Bosnia and Herzegovina as well as Croatia have experienced similar developments. The role of NGOs in cultural activities has been constantly growing, which strongly influenced and in many cases enabled cultural creativity and support to individual artists. At the same time, cultural products have entered the emerging and not well-organized cultural markets.

The establishment and elaboration of public cultural policies in all Southeast European countries have continuously enjoyed professional and financial support offered by the Council of Europe through the *European Program of*

Evaluation of National Cultural Policies which started in 1986 and is still going on. Quite diversified, these policies have been formulated by state ministries. They have helped a (re)structuration of national cultural spaces, preserved financing and functioning of cultural institutions and raised the awareness of culture as social value. However, their impacts on cultural creativity and cultural exchange remain limited. It has become evident by now that the cultural NGO sector, its supporters and new cultural markets visibly influence the present day development of Southeast European cultures as these become ever more open to exchange and communication within the global context.

Globalization and Globalism

Globalization has been generally understood as an all-inclusive process that has embraced all types of human activity across the world. Among countless definitions that have emerged from the descriptions and analyses of globalization, the following one seems to express the nature of globalization most adequately for the purposes of the following analysis: "... globalization is best seen as a multidimensional and multidirectional process involving accelerated and increased flows of virtually everything—capital, commodities, information, ideas, beliefs, people—along constantly evolving axes" (UNESCO 2009:5).

Globalization, described and understood as a multidimensional and multidirectional process, has created a state of globalism. Globalism is often interpreted as a new historical paradigm that sees a networked interactive cultural environment emerging from global economic, technological, and social processes. Such an environment strongly supports the creation of new globalized cultural contexts characterized by intensive cultural communication, and this currently is true of most living cultures. The possibility to experience different cultures deepens the knowledge of the values they have developed over time. Through intercultural communication cultural borders have become elusive, flexible, and open (Švob-Dokić 2006:8; 2008:238). The original cultural varieties are now relatively easily transferred, used and practiced in very different cultural contexts, which may subject them to different interpretations and different usages. As cultures are increasingly linked by networked communication (Benkler 2006; Castells 2009), they are exposed to the fast and effective exchange of content, values, symbols, meanings, and cultural products, which have all become relatively easily accessible due to new technological developments and, in particular, the Internet.

95

This constantly increasing cultural exchange and communication has strongly influenced the character and position of national cultures. Their role in globalization processes has been largely discussed during the past about 30 years. The particular positions of specific cultures have been reflected in their involvement "in the movement of specified objects, systems of meaning and people across national/regional borders and continents" (Anheier and Raj Isar 2007:9). Specific cultures participate in globalization processes in different ways; they either passively accept various globalization trends or invest efforts to actively adapt and involve themselves in such processes. In this way they initiate cultural transitions that enable their participation in cultural globalization trends. Such participation is reflected in the constantly growing cultural exchange and communication, which results in the change of the structures, social positions and creative potentials of the national, mostly European, cultures.

These national cultures display relatively basic structures. They originated within the developing nation states in the 18th, 19th, and 20th centuries. The cultural identification processes typical of national cultures were based on the integration of various pre-national cultures, cultural values, and cultural practices, and strongly linked to the newly established national language and artistic practices. Today these processes have become increasingly dependent on local cultures and their specificities, on the (re)interpretation of cultural heritage, and on local cultural products and cultural industries (Potts 2011). They have been encouraged to adapt to global communication processes and to cultural exchange through global markets. In order to be globally exchangeable, they need to observe certain production and technological standards so as to participate in less territorialized cultural production, innovation, and creativity. While the increased economic exchange of cultural values and goods again involves a certain standardization of production processes and products, the state of cultural globalism that prompts local responses tends to support individualized and de-standardized innovative cultural products and to increase their variety and variability. The ensuing cultural dynamics support innovation and generate the need to reinterpret cultural originality and original cultural artifacts and values, leading to the development of new, a-national cultures.

Cultures everywhere have always been diverse and increasingly diversified through mutual contacts. However, for a certain period of time, national cultures displayed relatively harmonized structures with an established and observed hierarchy of values and types of sectorial cultural products which were transparent. This may be best illustrated by the efforts invested in a successful standardization of national languages, which enabled functional communication within national borders. Artistic productions tended to be aimed at people with more cultivated tastes and this became the standardized framework for communication between general audiences and artists. More or less harmonized behavioral values enabled the generalized and widely accepted evaluation of various cultural products, but also helped artists and creators to pursue more individual ideas, and their creativity resulted in the development of new cultural values and meanings. Cultures used to be financed nationally, either through public funds or individual donations, always promoting the cultural values as public values.

Today such a national structure of cultures is being dissolved. In parallel, attitudes toward culture and the arts are changing and are evolving toward deinstitutionalization of cultural productivity and individualization of cultural consumption. Contemporary cultures have been actively included and exposed to radical changes in cultural production, which could symbolically be interpreted as a transition from the national to the global cultural contexts that are being re-created through the interaction of cultural creativity with all other human activities. In the process, the notion of culture has widened and has become almost all-encompassing. In this respect Terry Eagleton (2005:31, 40) notes that a critical self-reflection of culture makes it inclusive of practically everything ("...lust, arts, language, media, body, gender, ethnicity...").

As globalization has activated the restructuring of national cultures, it has become possible to understand its dynamics and some of the outcomes of the ongoing cultural changes. The national and global contexts have provided a framework for a new cultural environment symbolized by a notion of cultural space (Harvey 2006). The concept of a specialized space (Storper 1997:19-44) and the concept of a cultural space (Švob-Đokić 2008:238) are derived from analyses of cultural globalization (Beck and Grande 2012), understood as an ongoing process that is open to creative efforts expressed through symbolic signs and content. Various possible interpretations of culture are not made more complicated by these concepts, but they substantiate its existence, presence, and development in a certain socio-historical reality and thus, in practice, reduce a vaguely defined cultural all-inclusiveness to a certain reality, today called globalism.

Cultural spaces are defined by flexible imaginary aspects (artistic, creative, anthropological, linguistic, and other, Appadurai 1998); they are constructed to help the contextualization of human existence within some space that is a-territorial and embraces both virtual and value aspects of cultures. Cultures interact with physical spaces through creativity and step outside their own spaces through communication that provokes dynamic changes to all cultural spaces and to the values they may contain.

The temporal/historical processes (Harvey 2006) testify to the fact that cultural spaces are continuously constructed and deconstructed. In contemporary Europe these processes have been reflected in the structured national cultures that have developed a set of standardized cultural values, languages, arts, and types of behavior, which have contributed to the establishment of general social settings. National cultures are normally subjected to certain dynamics of inner development, which are reflected in changes to values and to other cultural elements. Over time they develop and host various types of cultural product, consumption, and exchange, which continuously promote cultural change leading to the deconstruction of established cultural structures and the values supporting these structures. In present-day Europe, a prevailing type of national culture is being deconstructed in the context of globalism through dynamic cultural transition. This is the result of cultural industrialization and the emergence of new types of cultural values and products which are developed through the usage of new technologies and the general systemic social changes that are now particularly visible in the post-communist countries.

The state of globalism offers new contextual surroundings for the continuity of construction and deconstruction of cultural spaces, cultures, and cultural policies. So far it has influenced and enabled the stratification of the established national cultures and brought new challenges for contemporary cultural policies, which have previously been institutionalized as national, local, or city public policies. Such different types and aspects of cultural stratification are interconnected or even integrated by a holistic view of cultures as complex, innovative, and adaptive value systems, able to meet various cultural sensitivities, tastes, and traditions.

Cultural Spaces and the Emerging Types of Stratified National Culture
The processes of cultural stratification within standardized national cultures in Europe, and in Southeast Europe in particular , have led to the following types of cultural entity (Švob-Dokić 2012).

Institutional culture is based on state-supported cultural institutions (such as museums, libraries, national theatres, orchestras, and others) that mostly depend on public financial sources. Cultural institutions largely reflect the establishment and development of nation states and state cultural policies which may have been recently decentralized to the local and city levels. Institutional culture is primarily concentrated on the establishment, definition, and preservation of national cultural values which have become "traditional." These values are interpreted as being in keeping with ideas of national cultural identity and they enable and preserve its development. In this respect the preservation of cultural heritage and the (often hasty) representation of authentic cultural values are of key interest. Such interest is sustained and boosted through international cultural cooperation, the organization of cultural events and festivals, and other cultural activities representing national creativity and values. Investment in culture is primarily directed to institutions and cultural infrastructure, but this does not imply that they are being restructured or modernized; it simply secures their survival in the changing social surroundings, often at a high cost. The existing cultural institutions have difficulty in adapting to the globalized cultural communication. They can barely sustain and support cultural creativity. In this sense they prove to be dysfunctional and dependent on obsolete concepts and programs which often result in a lowering of their professional standards and the expulsion of the best artists or other creative professionals. These, particularly in the case of post-communist countries, often take their chances abroad. Those cultural institutions that are able and ready to invest time and effort in adapting to new social contexts and demands earn the position of protected cultural institutions, and are preserved as part of national traditions and cultural heritage.

Independent culture has been developing through transitional processes, as a kind of intermediary creative activity that grows through networking and the use of new communication technologies. This is usually financially supported by international organizations and foundations which may be either private (e.g., the Open Society/Soros Foundations) or public (e.g., the European Cultural Foundation). The "independent" culture functions mostly through nongovernmental organizations and individual small enterprises. It is able to attract an important number of creative individuals and to invest both funds and effort in local cultural creativity. As the international financial sources are being reduced over time, the "independent" culture tends to turn increasingly to local public funds (which introduces a threat of political influence) and to various private sources seeking to avoid the cultural marketplace. Such intentions are reflected in efforts to institutionalize cultural activities and thus change cultural mainstreams, sensitivities, and values. The "independent" culture is present in public life through modern art, new dance trends, experiments in theatre, and also often through developments in design, fashion, and other brands of modern artistic and cultural industrial creativity. It is able to accept, introduce, and reinterpret global creative trends at local levels, to work with new technologies and communicate globally. Although its treatment of cultural industries is distrustful due to its unwillingness to turn to the markets, its products are close to those of cultural industries and pop art, particularly as regards music and audiovisual work. This culture addresses large audiences and it refuses to accept an elitist social status.

Market-oriented culture operates internationally in both global and local cultural markets. It follows pop-cultural consumerism and often domesticates and imitates global trends in pop-music, for instance through the organization of cultural events such as large concerts and festivals, and participates regularly in the development of cultural industries. The cultural communication that it develops is based on the format of business interests. Market-oriented cultural products are sponsored by big companies and other sponsors who are not interested in program and content but who appreciate the quality and popularity of cultural products and, in particular, their attractiveness to large audiences. As this sort of culture boosts cultural markets, it enjoys a kind of creative freedom and draws profits from the increasing consumption of its products. The market-oriented culture is open to very different types of cultural creativity and it is able to offer good cultural products from any origin. In an effort to meet market demands it is totally dependent on industrialized, reproductive, and repetitive cultural production, namely on cultural industries.

If the presumption that a number of European national cultures display similar structures is correct, the spatial reach of the identified cultural types might be pan-European, but not always typical of each particular culture. The structural analysis of contemporary cultural spaces that include different stratified cultures demands the development of a global structure that would encompass cultural diversity, multiculturalism, and intercultural dialogue as constituent elements of any type of contemporary national culture and the eventual cultural space in which it exists. In order to include numerous diverse and varied aspects of these potential cultural spaces in the context of globalism, cultural policy needs to concentrate almost exclusively on the communication, exchange, and cooperation among existing cultures and on the technological infrastructures that can enable the networking and interlinking of cultural spaces. The analytical attempts to design such an approach to culture have so far included interpretations of notions such as *world culture, transnational culture, global culture,* and *global multiculture.*

Ulf Hannerz (1996:106) defines world culture as "an organized diversity" that is interconnected by the universality of cultural values. The concept of transnational culture interprets cultural borders as distinctive and the need to overcome them as a call for tolerance and understanding of others (Robins 2006). Jan Nederveen Pieterse (2007) sees cultural pluralism as a basis for the concept of global multiculture. It is derived from elements of ethnicity, multiethnicity, and multiculturalism that are encompassed by cultural globalism. However, cultural development and the role of cultural policies in this respect have not been extensively analyzed in the light of cultural productivity that might stream from intercultural communication within the context of globalism.

The identified cultural types reflect an inner developmental dynamics of national cultures (Švob-Đokić et al. 2014). Exposed to global influences they are changing identities through new types of cultural creativity and mutual connectivity. These incite national cultures to overstep their national boundaries and participate actively in cultural globalization trends. As the context of globalism has not yet been fully structured, the cultural re-identification processes might influence its formation by implanting a number of specialized cultural production areas.

A Case Illustrating the Stratification of a National Culture: Croatia

The identification of Croatian culture as "national" is associated with the libertarian bourgeois movements in mid-19th century and cultural and historical developments in the first half of 20th century, particularly those related to the First and Second World Wars.

The understanding of Croatian culture has evolved from romantic interpretations of culture as a framework for the standardization of Croatian language and identification of cultural heritage as "Croatian" to the inclusion of artistic production and creativity (plastic and fine arts, music, literature) into European traditions and the literary and artistic movements of the time. A view of culture as a comprehensive value system, as a type of production, and creativity has evolved by the mid-20th century, particularly with the development of film industry, audiovisual production, and modern arts. Technological advances became ever more influential and supportive of intensive cultural exchange and communication. Mediation of cultural communication largely contributed to cultural exchange. Notwithstanding the ups and downs of cultural development, the role of the state, formatted by both historical and political as well as European and global cultural influences, has been established as crucial. The state (whether independent republic or a republic within Yugoslavia) was in a position to either support or prevent certain types of cultural creativity. Its role deeply impacted the recent systemic cultural transition through the establishment and development of a cultural policy.

The re-definition of national culture, strong mediation, and mediatization of cultural creativity and the revision of cultural policy focused on Croatian cultural resources are seen here through the lens of cultural globalization and in the context of cultural globalism. Processes of re-definition of the Croatian national culture are here illustrated by changes of the concept of culture, changes in cultural communication, and by an overall reorientation of cultural policy.

The concept of culture. The holistic concept of Croatian national culture (identified through language, cultural inheritance, and types of cultural creativity) was slowly disintegrated through its modernization, re-identification, and openness to strong global technological influences in the framework of transitional processes. The initial understanding of culture remained based in the specialized activities supposed to constitute an interactive area of creativity: literature, plastic and fine arts, music, and other cultural branches. Such specialized fields are still operational and preserved as types of programs included within the institutional culture. The budget of the Ministry of Culture (Budget, Program Shares 2015) identifies the following cultural activity areas and their budget shares: management of culture (8% of the current budget), museums and galleries (10%), theaters and music (15%), libraries and printing industries (6%), audiovisuals and the media (8%), archives (9%), preservation of cultural heritage (26%), and other cultural activities (18%).

This split of supported programs reflects an understanding of culture as a sum of specialized cultural activities. The limited number of areas leaves a number of other creative and cultural activities and specializations aside and thus limits the understanding of culture to the concept of *institutional culture*, that is, the culture managed by the state. However, global cultural influences have largely widened the perceptions of cultural specializations and fields. They have introduced new interpretations of culture as "a critical self-reflection" that "makes it inclusive of practically everything" (Eagleton 2005:31). This is also connected with the anthropological understanding of culture as "a way of life." The understanding of culture as an all-encompassing holistic area of life and creativity has supported a structural diversification of the cultural field, which is reflected in the growth of independent culture and the establishment of specialized cultural organizations, such as *POGON* — Zagreb center for independent culture and youth; *Kulturpunkt* (NGO Kurziv — The platform for issues of culture, media and society), cultural and dance centers and others. In 2011 the *Kultura Nova Foundation* dedicated to the development and co-financing of independent cultural scene was established (Zaklada Kultura nova 201. Ninety-three cultural NGOs active in different cultural fields are now registered in Croatia (Barada, Primorac, and Buršić 2016). As a result of systemic transition and diversified cultural consumption, a specialized cultural market has emerged and became clearly visible.

Cultural communication and the media. Global cultural influences have been largely transferred through printed and digitalized media. Easily accessible contents have met local interests in all cultural activities and expressions. As the media have generated processes of mediation and mediatization of culture (Hepp 2013) they have also included local networks in the distribution of cultural products.

All three identified types of the Croatian national culture have been submitted to strong interactive relations with different media. The contextualization of the media and the issuing processes of mediatization indicate that the role of different media in cultural mediatization is different, and that the results of media involvement in the cultural production and consumption are different. The varieties of such influences and impacts depend on the type of the media and on the cultural type and they produce a number of new cultural specializations embracing life styles, cooking, fashion, and interest in "traditional" cultural productions such as classical music, painting, and other.

Institutional culture is mediated and mediatized through the creation of information on the cultural production, organization, and functioning of cultural institutions. It often represents artists and their works and achievements, cultural activists and professionals, workers and managers who are in the most cases fully employed by cultural organizations and institutions (e.g., museums, orchestras, theatres, etc.). The information on cultural activities is produced by professionals employed either in the Ministry of Culture or by media organizations. Mediation mostly refers to the established print and electronic media organized under the principles of the mass media communication. The extension (Schulz 2004) of cultural information may take place online through websites of the established media organizations.

Independent culture is influenced by the media and mediatized through cultural activities (publishing, theater performances, film making, exhibitions, etc.) which are usually communicated online. Cultural creativity is deterritorialized, organized through projects, networked, and mostly virtual. The social position of cultural workers is not quite transparent. Communication depends on the interested public and may be quite restricted to the particular groups. The presentation and mediatization of this type of culture depends on the virtual and networked individual communication much more than on the institutionalized mass communication media. It is not submitted to the established professional standards, but rather follows creative interests of either educated or devoted public. Such communication may be quite flexible and open as it is only occasionally included in the processes of professional mediation by critics or the institutionalized media. This type of mediated communication provides for new values and highly individualized inspiration. It may be expressed in new productive efforts inclined toward the mediatization of cultural creativity.

Market-oriented culture uses the inspiration for cultural creativity and cultural products (that come from either institutional or independent culture) to place them on the market. This mostly takes place through the creation of cultural events, popular concerts, or popular performances. The cultural products may be re-packaged in order to become easily consumable. The communication of the contents and events within this cultural type are generally virtualized, and may be mediated through the TV, radio, and products of the cultural industries. The cultural production and consumption within this cultural type is clearly territorialized (in public premises, city squares, TV studios, etc.) but it nevertheless reaches large audiences. The mediatized cultural communication is largely shaped by, and oriented toward market logics.

The Croatian culture has been diversified according to the production, distribution, consumption, the use of cultural products, and the specific mode of cultural communication developed through the distribution and consumption. The presence and the role of the media depend at the same time and equally on their character and the general interests of specific media in cultural themes and issues. Moreover, the cultural production and cultural communication shaped by various media interact to generate mediatization processes. These are related to traditional mass communication abilities as well as to the mediatized connectivity, and may be organized by either established media organizations or by interested individuals. In this respect, "Mediatization…refers to the process of construction of socio-cultural reality by communication" and, "…in turn, existing specifics of certain media have a contextualized 'influence' on the process of communicative construction of socio-cultural reality" (Hepp and Krotz 2014:3).

The structural analysis of contemporary cultural spaces opens the possibility to discuss specific characteristics of the Croatian culture as constituent elements of "*long term structural* transformations of the relation between media and modern society at large" (Hjarvard 2014:125). These "long term structural transformations" within the Croatian national culture indicate that there is certain compatibility between cultural types and the related media types. Such compatibility largely defines their interactions and the issuing communicative construction of the mediatized cultural realities that are strongly influenced by the cultural globalism and globalization of culture.

The identified Croatian cultural types are the result of ongoing wider social transformation processes, that is, of the transition from socialism to capitalism and of strong external globalization influences. Interactions among media and cultural productions, cultural creativity, and consumption are clearly visible in each identified cultural type. The parallel impacts of the media are reflected in the mediatized communication that has deeply influenced all these structural transformations and clearly indicated the existing and preferable relations between the types of media and the identified cultural types. Although culturally contextualized in all three identified cultural types, the processes of mediatization have nevertheless remained fluid and difficult to systematize.

Cultural policy. "In the early 1990s, the cultural policy of independent Croatia was politically and administratively centralized … with special emphasis on national traditions" (Primorac, Obuljen Koržinek, and Švob-Đokić 2014:2). The priority was given to "national interest" while the policy issues were formulated in rather general terms, "emphasizing market approach, freedom of creativity and professionalism."

Efforts to further organize national cultural activities and deepen the elaboration of cultural policy issues were introduced through the inclusion of Croatia into the *European Program of Evaluation of National Cultural Policies* (Cvjetičanin and Katunarić 1999). The Croatian Ministry of Culture supported expert teams whose mission was to explicitly standardize Croatian cultural policy with European and global policy trends. A more balanced approach to cultural traditions, cultural pluralism, and multiculturalism was in line with the cultural reality of Croatia, and it was organizationally supported by the decentralization of cultural activities and public financial sources. This was reflected in the split of the public financing of culture, which was continuously decreasing. In 2013 the Ministry of Culture accounted for 38% of the public expenditure for culture, the share of towns, including the capital was 54%; while the participation of counties and municipalities was only 8% (Primorac, Obuljen Koržinek, and Švob-Ðokić 2014:42, 43). Cooperation with a dynamically growing "independent" NGOs cultural sector, subsidized mostly by foreign foundations, was established.

The general objectives of cultural policy (such as observance of aesthetic and multiethnic cultural pluralism, creative autonomy, polycentric cultural development, cooperation between the public and the private sector and others) were proclaimed. These coincided with the cultural policy aims in most countries—48 signatory members of the Council of Europe—and reflected the intensions and efforts to integrate the Croatian cultural development into the frameworks of European cultures and cultural policies.

The Croatia in the 21st Century: Strategy of Cultural Development (Cvjetičanin and Katunarić 2003), passed in the Croatian Parliament in 2002, proclaimed an overall goal of Croatian cultural development: the democratization of culture. This goal was also supported by legal provisions and policy instruments such as the distribution of funds. It resulted in a continuously increasing cultural and media openness and communication, in growing bilateral and multilateral cultural cooperation, and in initial links between publicly supported and "independently" or privately subsidized cultural programs and projects. Cultural policy became better structured and more transparent.

Globalizing influences on such tendencies have been particularly visible in a growing interest in and openness toward new contents and genres (e.g., in plastic arts, theatrical experiments, modern dance, a hasty development of TV series, and others), in mediated and mediatized cultural values, contents, activities, and creativity; in an initial development of cultural industries and industrialization of cultural production, including design, fashion, and other; in emerging specialized, but small and fragile, cultural markets and the use of new technologies in cultural production. Notwithstanding the transfer of cultural policy standards, the cultural policy in Croatia remained focused on the institutionalized national and local levels and hardly interested in rationalizing the global influences.

Cultural Policies' Responses to Cultural Stratification

In the aforementioned interpretations of cultural globalism, the role and position of cultural policies have not been fully addressed. Although cultural policies have experienced changes in their roles, functioning, and scope, they are not quite adapted to the ongoing cultural stratification that has occurred through cultural development formatted by globalism and globalized cultural contexts and that is largely influenced by the still ongoing globalization processes. Cultural policies have diversified and expanded into different cultural strata and various cultural organizations, but remain feebly interlinked and mainly un-systematized.

In the *institutional culture*, the position and functioning of cultural policies have been best preserved. Within this type of culture cultural institutions are well established and their functioning is organized and planned by the state administration. Even when decentralized to the local and city levels, cultural policies follow general administrative, organizational, and financial rules. Moreover, they remain "…oriented primarily toward supporting supply side, while the demand side (users' expectations and needs) that points to the relevance of cultural offer in the present day context to the present day audience has not been tackled adequately" (Primorac, Obuljen Koržinek, and Uzelac 2015:17). Cultural production within such frameworks may be repetitive, but it clearly reflects standards of creativity and consumption developed in line with the standards set by the state and by national cultural identification frameworks. In this sense, it widely supports cultural professionalism and is interested in presenting its results internationally.

The *independent culture* is supported by foundations, whether private or public, and follows manifold and multidirectional aims. Cultural policy is eventually developed by very different NGOs or professional cultural and media associations, as well as by individual small enterprises. At the same time the frameworks for cultural production and creativity are designed by the interested sponsors, often in cooperation with the artists and producers concerned. The need for flexibility and temporary orientations in creativity and production mean that planning and relative stability in cultural creativity are rare. This prevents stable financing of cultural actions and programs. Participants in independent culture accept such risks and short-term projects that may have very interesting results, or may fail. Professionalism is rarely seen as a value; instead, inspiration, and approval of outcomes that may shock are valued. In this respect the actors of independent culture rely increasingly on co-creative projects (e.g., in film industry). A visible orientation to an eventual policy approach is focused on co-production, cooperation, and communication among involved actors.

Market-oriented culture is clearly governed by the rules of the market. The "invisible hand of the market" organizes cultural and artistic professionals and creators and follows just one rule: profit making. Artistic and cultural creativity produces quick results, and there are no limits to either professional or value considerations. The interaction with various audiences is intensive and momentary, rapidly negotiated, and responsive to all kinds of sensitivities. Cultural policies only relate to temporary projects with limited content, and to technological innovations that may support cultural consumption. In practical terms, cultural policy appears to be a policy of response to market interests, which also includes the attempt to adapt or even change the structure and character of cultural markets.

The interactions among the identified cultural strata and cultural policies developed within them are not clearly visible. It is not entirely clear what links could be established among different strata, and how. Processes of cultural policy making do not provide for better communication and interaction among different cultural strata, and cultural policy making remains strongly connected to the role of the state (Hartley et al. 2013:69–73) within the institutional culture. Policy actors within the independent and market-oriented culture are less transparent and less interested in defining any cultural policy.

A certain proliferation of cultural policies is, however, visible at the level of cultural organizations, associations, networks, cultural industries, and cities and regions. They each formulate some kind of cultural policy for themselves and their needs, and there is no visible interlinking of such policies. Even if, and when, the state offers some support to the activities of these organizations as part of the defined aims of cultural policies, this does not lead to processes that may help to standardize or systematize a large number of specialized cultural policies. In this respect, cultural policy has been reduced to an instrument (often identified with "cultural strategy") that may eventually be useful, but that may serve very different aims. The development of such an instrument may be supported by national state aid or investment, but this is not offered permanently and cannot reach a large number of cultural organizations and cultural industries. Many among them also do not want to lose their relatively independent autonomous positions, their opportunities to function flexibly, and to develop programs and activities that they can direct at various audiences through different markets.

Even if cultural stratification in Southeast European culture is not always fully transparent and even if cultures do not always display the same cultural subtypes, they do reflect processes of cultural deinstitutionalization and the general transformation of attitudes toward culture. In relation to cultural spaces, cultural policies have been only partly de- and re-constructed, and this has intensified discussions about their nature, scope, and functioning. In a way, the concept of national culture has been dissolved within the concept of cultural space, but this also remains rather vague. As cultural dynamics reflect the increase in cultural production, exchange and communication, and the intensity of cultural exchanges, cultural policies can be slow to adapt to the state of globalism that is reflected in a wider and not clearly defined notion of cultural space. Although cultural policies remain predominantly confined to national cultural spaces and to the strata of institutionalized cultures, they increasingly need to conceptualize various possible types of cultural surroundings and spaces, which might help them to adapt and thus to improve their functioning and flexibility.

In the context of globalism, cultural policies might encourage ideas of democratic governance to be introduced within cultural spaces. They may strengthen relationships between local and national cultural policy levels and reflect both global and local influences on cultural policy making. However, the relationship between cultural policies and markets that demand liberalized cultural exchanges in the context of globalism remains undefined. There is a divergence between the interests of publicly supported cultural institutions, workers, and artists on the one hand, and consumers as individual users of cultural goods and values on the other.

The question is whether the transformation of cultural policies through the enlargement of their scope to global surroundings (Kleberg 2002) might be possible. When they refer strictly to the institutionalized (and state-supported) culture they diminish their scope, and their functionality is reduced even if such policies may be reproduced and adapted to local cultures at subnational or regional levels. When the existing national policies refer to globalized contexts, as for example in the case of audiovisual productions, their role is restricted and minor in comparison to market influences, technological prerogatives, or policies of large integrations such as the European Union. Moreover, their possibility to integrate into global markets is vulnerable both conceptually and financially. This is, for example, seen when cultural policies support specialized cultural networks that integrate cultural agents through projects and defined tasks which need not be influenced by state cultural interests (Švob-Đokić 2011). Networks remain far more flexible, often less professional and less permanent, which limits possible cultural policy influences on them. Furthermore, the notion of cultural space scarcely contextualizes the possibilities for cultural policies to function at horizontal local, national, and regional levels. In this sense, the here identified cultural stratification remains almost untouched by national cultural policies and their outcomes at either local or regional levels.

A Concluding Note

In an effort to trace the recent processes of cultural change in Southeast European post-socialist countries, a type of cultural stratification driven by global influences is identified as an indicator of new cultural settings and of redefined cultural spaces. The context of globalism and global influences are supportive of a holistic concept that sees culture as a complex, innovative, and adaptive system of values, not strictly limited by state borders. In this respect impacts of new technologies and intensive cultural communication are particularly valued. Global influences inspire an inner restructuration of national cultures and directly affect their structures. Such restructuration is generally reflected in: constantly increasing and intensive cultural exchange empowered by new technologies and the media; technological impacts on cultural production and creativity particularly visible in the development of cultural and creative industries; permanent growth of cultural distribution and consumption of cultural products, connected to the emergence and development of cultural markets; and, in an increased participation in culture, particularly through the processes of co-creativity. Moreover, these global influences are ever more reflected in cultural creativity and new types of cultural sensitivity, which is particularly sustained by individual artists and, in organizational sense, by NGOs devoted to cultural activities.

The response of the newly established cultural policies to such new cultural developments may be crucial. However the Southeast European cultural policies are only partly responding to the new challenges of cultural growth and restructuration. Their focus remains within the concept of a national culture, diversified by regional and local cultures and influences, but not oriented to the wider global cultural scope. In this respect, the efforts have been invested in addressing culture as a resource that influences social cohesion, increases knowledge of different cultures, and promotes identity aspects. It can be said that the attempts by cultural policies to adapt to the state of globalism have been weak and not fully transparent. Their adaptation to globalism may have turned them into not quite clearly defined instruments that may have potential to mainstream creativity into cultural and art production, which may help the positioning of a culture in the global cultural space and context. At the same time Southeast European cultural policies largely miss an orientation to programs that focus on cultural production, innovation, smart specialization, cultural trade, intellectual property regulation, and other globally relevant issues.

The case of Croatian culture illustrates well the position of a culture fully exposed to the European and global cultural influences. It exists in between the efforts to preserve some of its own traditions and values on one side, and to adapt to global cultural exchange and communication on the other. In the global context the success or failure of such adaptation is an issue of creativity and innovation.

References

Andreeva, Diana, and Bilyana Tomova. (2011) Bulgaria. In *Council of Europe/ ERICarts Compendium: Cultural Policies and Trends in Europe*. 16th edition. <http://www.culturalpolicies.net/web/Bulgaria.php>.

Anheier, Helmut, and Isar, (Raj) Yudhishthir. (2007) Introducing the Cultures and Globalization Series. In *The Cultures and Globalization Series 1: Conflicts and Tensions*, eds. Helmut Anheier, and Raj Yudhishthir Isar, 3-16. London: Sage.

Appadurai, Arjun. (1998) *Modernity At Large: Cultural Dimensions of Globalization*. Minneapolis: University of Minnesota Press.

Balsan, Bianca-Maria. (2012) Romania. In *Council of Europe/ERICarts Compendium: Cultural Policies and Trends in Europe*. 16th edition. <http://www. culturalpolicies.net/web/Romania.php>.

Barada, Valerija, Jaka Primorac, and Edgar Buršić. (2016) *Osvajanje prostora rada.* (Taking over the space of work) Zagreb: Biblioteka Kultura nova.

Beck, Ulrich, and Edgar Grande. (2012) Standard article. In *The Wiley-Blackwell Encyclopedia of Globalization*, ed. George Ritzer, Wiley Online Library, John Wiley and Sons, Inc. Chichester, West Sussex and Malden MA DOI: 101002/9780470670590.wbeog583.

Benkler, Yoshua. (2006) *The Wealth of Networks: How Social Production Transforms Markets and Freedom*. New Haven, London: Yale University Press.

Castelles, Manuel. (2009) *Communication Power*. Oxford, New York: Oxford University Press.

Council of Europe. (1986–2016) *The European Program of Evaluation of National Cultural Policies*. <www.coe.int/t/dg4/cultureheritage/culture/ Reviews/Default_en.asp> (Accessed 28 May 2016).

Cvjetičanin, Biserka, and Vjeran Katunarić, eds. (1999) *The Cultural Policy of the Republic of Croatia.* National Report. Council of Europe: The European Program of Evaluation of National Cultural Policies. Strasbourg/Zagreb: The Ministry of Culture of the Republic of Croatia.

Cvjetičanin, Biserka, and Vjeran Katunarić, eds. (2003) *Hrvatska u 21.stoljeću. Strategija kulturnog razvitka*. Dokument. (Croatia in the 21st century. The strategy of cultural development. Document). Zagreb: The Ministry of Culture of the Republic of Croatia.

Eagleton, Terry. (2005) *Teorija i nakon nje* (After Theory). Zagreb: Algoritam. Hannerz, Ulf. (1996) Transnational Connections: Culture, People, Places. London: Routledge.

Hartley, John, Jason Potts, Stuart Cunningham, Terry Flew, Michael Keane, and John Banks. (2013) Cultural Policy. In *Key Concepts in Creative Industries*, 69–73. Los Angeles, London, New Delhi, Singapore, Washington DC: Sage Publications Ltd.

Hartley, John, Wen Wen, and Henry Siling Li. (2015) *Creative Economy and Culture*. Los Angeles, London, New Delhi, Singapore, Washington DC: Sage.

Harvey, David. (2006/1990) *The Condition of Postmodernity. An Enquiry into the Origins of Cultural Change*. Malden: Blackwell Publishing.

Hepp, Andreas. (2013) *Cultures of Mediatization*. Cambridge: Polity Press.

Hepp, Andreas, and Friedrich Krotz. (2014) Mediatized Worlds— Understanding Everyday Mediatization. In *Mediatized Worlds. Culture and Society in a Media Age*, eds. Andreas Hepp, and Friedrich Krotz, 1–15. Houndmills: Palgrave Macmillan.

Hjarvard, Stig. (2014) From Mediation to Mediatization: The Institutionalization of New Media. In *Mediatized Worlds. Culture and Society in a Media Age*, eds. Andreas Hepp, and Friedrich Krotz, 123–139. Houndmills: Palgrave Macmillan.

Kleberg, Carl-Johan. (2002) National Cultural Policy Reviews: A Method to Discuss and Improve Cultural Policies. Paper presented at The Second International Conference on Cultural Policy Research, Wellington, New Zealand.

Ministry of Culture of the Republic of Croatia. (2015) Budget 2015: Program shares. <www.min-kulture.hr> (Accessed 26 January 2016).

Nederveen Pieterse, Jan. (2007) *Ethnicities and Global Multiculture: Pants for an Octopus*. Lanham, Boulder, New York, Toronto, Plymouth, UK: Rowman and Littlefield Publishers, Inc.

Potts, Jason. (2011) Creative Industries and Economic Evolution. Cheltenham: Edward Elgar.

Primorac, Jaka, Nina Obuljen Koržinek, and Aleksandra Uzelac. (2015) Access to Culture in Croatian Cultural Policy: Moving Towards Explicit Policies. *International Journal of Cultural Policy*. <http://www.tandfonline.com/eprint/WSznhGjBXQ8MWYhr/full> (Accessed 2 February 2016).

Primorac, Jaka, Nina Obuljen Koržinek, and Nada Švob-Đokić. (2014) *Compendium of Cultural Policies and Trends in Europe — Croatia*. 16th edition. Council of Europe/ERICarts. <http://www.culturalpolicies.net> (Accessed 28 January 2016).

Robins, Kevin. (2006) *The Challenge of Transcultural Diversities. Transversal Study on the Theme of Cultural Policy and Cultural Diversity.* Strasbourg: Council of Europe Publishing.

Schulz, Winfried. (2004) Reconstructing Mediatization as an Analytical Concept. *European Journal of Communication* 19 (1): 87–101.

Storper, Michael. (1997) Territories, Flows and Hierarchies in the Global Economy. In *Spaces of Globalization. Reasserting the Power of the Local*, ed. Robert Cox, 19–44. New York, London: The Guilford Press.

Švob-Đokić, Nada. (2006) *New Borders and the Borderless Cultures. In Dynamics of Communication: New Ways and New Actors*, ed. Biserka Cvjetičanin, 5–12. Zagreb: Institute for International Relations.

Švob-Đokić, Nada. (2008) *Open Cultural Spaces in Search of New Frontiers*. Revista CIDOB d'Affers Internacionals 82-83 (9): 237–244.

Švob-Đokić, Nada. (2011) Cultural Networks and Cultural Policies: A Missing Link. In *Networks: The Evolving Aspects of Culture in the 21st Century*, ed. Biserka Cvjetičanin, 25–30. Zagreb: Institute for International Relations.

Švob-Đokić, Nada. (2012) Cultural Networks and Imagined Regionalism. In *Towards Open Regionalism in Southeast Europe*, eds. Paul Stubbs, and Christophe Solioz, 117–131. Baden Baden: Nomos.

Švob-Đokić, Nada, Jeronim Dorotić, Dinko Klarić, and Nina Obuljen Koržinek. (2014) The Intercultural Dialogue in Croatia: Between Policies and Practices. In *Culture and Sustainable Development in the Times of Crisis*, eds. Milena Dragičević Šešić, Mirjana Nikolić, and Ljiljana Rogač Mijatović, 304–315. Belgrade: University of Arts in Belgrade, Faculty of Dramatic Arts and Institute for Theatre, Film, Radio and Television.

United Nations Educational, Scientific and Cultural Organization. (2009) UNESCO *World Report: Investing in Cultural Diversity and Intercultural Dialogue*. Executive Summary. Paris: UNESCO.

Zaklada Kultura nova. (2015) *Programski i financijski izvještaj za 2014*. Zagreb: Zaklada Kultura nova.

Theme 3:

Performance + Heritage

The Museum as a Transnational Actor

Patricia M. Goff

Patricia M. Goff is a Senior Fellow at the Centre for International Governance Innovation. She is also an associate professor of political science at Wilfrid Laurier University and the Balsillie School of International Affairs. Specializing in international political economy and international relations theory, she is the author of Limits of Liberalization: Local Culture in a Global Marketplace *and* Irrelevant or Indispensable?: The United Nations in the 21st Century.

Abstract

The museum has recently embarked on a new phase of transnational activity, marked by the establishment of international satellite branches. While it resembles for-profit and not-for-profit transnational actors in important ways, museum satellites are also unique in their motivation, impact, and partnerships. This observation can be a jumping off point for a new round of transnational actor theorizing that can accommodate entities like the museum.

Introduction

In the last 25 years, museums have opened satellite branches in international locations—the Guggenheim in Bilbao, Las Vegas, and Berlin; the Hermitage in Las Vegas and Amsterdam; and soon, possibly a Guggenheim in Helsinki and a Guggenheim and Louvre on Saadiyat Island in Abu Dhabi. For decades or longer, museums have participated in international exchanges or traveling exhibits of parts of their collections. In this respect, museums have long been active across borders. But, establishing a satellite branch is transnational activity of a different order. The branch strategy is driven by different motivations than the traditional art exchange and involves a different constellation of actors. Whereas art exchanges are typically effectuated between museums, establishing a foreign branch usually (though not always) implicates governments. Satellite branches can exercise distinct forms of political, cultural, and commercial power, making the museum relevant to scholars of global politics in a new way.[1]

In particular, satellite branches draw our attention to the museum as a distinctive transnational actor. It resembles many other transnational actors in *some* ways. Nonetheless, it fits uncomfortably into any standard category that we use to understand transnational activity. Situating the museum as a transnational actor is made more challenging by the fact that the drivers, mode of execution, objectives, and consequences of existing satellites are not identical to each other. Anecdotally, by way of example, one can point to the fact that the Guggenheim is a private museum, while the Hermitage and the Louvre are both quasi-public. What kind of transnational actor, then, is the museum? This article offers an exploration of the museum based on the typology of transnational actors that dominates debates in International Relations.

The one entity that most closely resembles the museum as a transnational actor is the university, which has also taken its transnational activity to a new level, not just exchanging faculty and students as it has long done, but also making its curriculum available digitally and opening branch campuses in far-flung locations. I flag it here to underline that understanding the transnational museum is intrinsically interesting in itself, but also indicative of a larger set of activities by transnational actors with unique economic, political, and ideational influence. Current transnational actor categories accommodate these new actors poorly.

[1] Museums have been amply studied by cultural studies, cultural policy, and urban planning but less so by IR scholars, with the exception of Christine Sylvester (2009).

This article proceeds in four parts. First, I describe the museum satellite phenomenon with special attention to the Guggenheim, Hermitage, and Saadiyat Island incarnations. Second, I explore why museums and their partners engage in this kind of transnational activity. Third, I attempt to situate the museum in the transnational actor categories on which we typically rely. The fourth section concludes.

The Phenomenon of the Museum Satellite

At this time, we can point to a handful of museum satellites that have come to fruition, but many more have been discussed or are under discussion, including Hermitage in Shanghai; Guggenheim in Guadalajara; British Museum and Victoria and Albert in China; Rodin Museum in Brazil; and Pompidou in Shanghai (Maher 2007). Several other museum branches have been established regionally. I will not discuss them here, but note that these include Pompidou Metz, Tate Britain, and Louvre Lens.

The Guggenheim

Before other museums followed suit, the satellite strategy was associated solely with the Guggenheim and, specifically, with Thomas Krens. Krens became the director of the Solomon R. Guggenheim Museum in New York in 1988 when the museum faced significant financial challenges (Guasch and Zulaika 2005:16). He initially sought to sell off some of the Guggenheim collection, but was criticized for this (MacCannell 2005:23). The International Council of Museums (ICOM) Code of Ethics suggests that such a practice is an inappropriate fund-raising activity as it may compromise the public trust in the museum's stewardship role (ICOM 2004). In 1990, Krens floated a $54.9 million bond issue, largely to finance a branch of the Guggenheim in SoHo, which ultimately failed (Haacke 2005:115). In the meantime, Krens had reportedly put out a number of feelers about possible international expansion sites, including in Salzburg, Berlin, and Madrid. While responses from these locations were luke warm, the city of Bilbao pursued the opportunity. A deal was struck in 1991 and the museum opened in 1997, touching off what many have termed "the Guggenheim Effect." The Guggenheim Bilbao is not just a museum, but an architectural landmark and a symbol of the city. It is tied to a strategy of urban renewal and has spurred tourism and economic growth.

The agreement between Krens and Bilbao emerged against the backdrop of Spanish politics in the 1970s and 1980s. The Basque Autonomous Region or Euskadi was created in 1979. In part, the Basque government sought to shift the depiction of the Basques as "the Indians of Europe" (MacCannell

119

2005:23). They soon also confronted serious economic challenges. Formerly home to thriving iron and steel mills, as well as mining, shipbuilding and a busy port, the region was undergoing deindustrialization by the mid-1980s. "The metropolitan area had lost 20% of its population and 47% of its industrial jobs in the two preceding decades" (Fraser 2005:47).

Economic woes were compounded by skittish investors who hesitated to put their money in a region known for Euskadi Ta Askatasuna (ETA) terrorist activity (Haacke 2005:118). At the same time, the region was aware of the need to find a meaningful identity within the growing European Union. These considerations led to a modernization and economic revitalization strategy to evolve from an industrial to a services city (Azua 2005:74). This plan presumed job creation, economic modernization, infrastructure development, increased tourism, and stimulus for local firms. Bilbao was the centerpiece of the regional strategy, which included a substantial cultural component.

Under the terms of the deal between the Basque Autonomous Government and the Guggenheim Museum, Krens asked for $20 million up front for the use of the Guggenheim name (Zulaika calls this the "franchise fee" (Zulaika 2005:150)); a commitment of an additional $100 million toward construction costs; $50 million for an art acquisition program; and an ongoing subsidy of $7 million per year for operating costs and maintenance (MacCannell 2005:23; see also Haacke 2005). More money would be forthcoming for acquisitions in later years (Haacke 2005:117). In return, the Guggenheim would offer its brand name, works from its collection, and travelling exhibitions. The Guggenheim retained complete control over programming, operations, and acquisitions. Bilbao would be the first experiment with a new strategy. "The Guggenheim's primary assets were its collection and its image.... instead of selling works from its collection, the museum hit on the idea of renting them—to itself. Branch museums financed by foreign governments and corporations, but directed entirely by management in New York, would pay the Guggenheim for the privilege of presenting its exhibitions and collections" (Fraser 2005:56).

Obviously, this was a huge risk on the part of the regional ministry of culture. It has paid off in many ways. "Immediately, the image of the Guggenheim became the international icon, displacing the ETA terrorist as the prime symbol of the region" (MacCannell 2005:24). From the first year, more than a million people have visited the museum annually, the vast majority from outside of Spain (MacCannell 2005:24). The Guggenheim Bilbao stimulated the Bilbao economy by bringing tourists and creating a need for cognate services. It also rebranded the city and the region from the seat of Basque terrorism and a deindustrialized economy to a must-see global cultural center. "Although interpretations of the numbers differ, the museum reportedly generated economic activity that added 47% to the gross regional product in its first year of operation, contributing to the maintenance of 3800 jobs, mostly through tourism" (Fraser 2005:51). Of course, the Bilbao experience has not been free of controversy. It has been criticized for promoting the Frank Gehry-designed building housing the art over the art itself. Also, while the Guggenheim museum gave Bilbao a foothold in the international art scene, it has arguably only stimulated the local arts community in limited ways. Some new arts institutions have grown up around the Guggenheim in its wake. However, the charge of "cultural imperialism" is enduring.

Few other Guggenheim satellites have taken hold like Bilbao. Helsinki and Abu Dhabi are in the relatively early stages, both plagued by controversy in different ways. The Berlin and Las Vegas ventures have long since closed their doors.[2] The Berlin Guggenheim dates to 1997 and a joint venture with Deutsche Bank. Krens had reportedly approached the bank a year earlier. He struck a deal with Hilmar Kopper, then president of the bank and chair of its supervisory board. The museum would be located in the bank's regional headquarters on the Unter den Linden in Berlin. The franchise would be called Deutsche Guggenheim. The terms of the Berlin deal remain a closely guarded secret (Haacke 2005:119). Kopper expressed the bank's rationale thusly: "Deutsche Guggenheim Berlin is an advertisement for Deutsche Bank's global expertise, quality, and innovative potential" (quoted in Haacke 2005:119). The space featured exhibitions from the Guggenheim and Deutsche bank collections, as well as commissioned works and works from international museums. The Deutsche Guggenheim officially closed in 2012. In its place is the Deutsche Bank KunstHalle, which continues to mount exhibitions that seem still to have a Guggenheim connection of some sort.[3]

[2] The Venice Guggenheim is the bequest of Peggy Guggenheim, opened in 1976. The collection is housed in the Palazzo Venier dei Leoni, where Peggy Guggenheim lived from 1949 until her death in 1979. Therefore, although the Venice satellite is a key location in the Guggenheim network, its existence did not come about as a result of the Krens satellite strategy.

The Guggenheim opened two branches in Las Vegas in 2001, both in the Venetian Hotel. The Guggenheim Las Vegas and the Guggenheim Hermitage were both designed by Rem Koolhaas. The Venetian paid for them, made other undisclosed contributions and shared operating income with the Guggenheim (Haacke 2005:121). Guggenheim Las Vegas closed after 18 months and one exhibition. The Guggenheim Hermitage closed in 2008. The Las Vegas Guggenheim branches were done in partnership with other cash-strapped museums, namely the Hermitage in St. Petersburg and the Kunsthistorisches Museum in Vienna. "Their ostensible common purpose is to mount shows from their respective collections in Las Vegas, Bilbao, New York, and in Venice, occasionally sponsored by Deutsche Bank" (Haacke 2005:121). The Berlin and Las Vegas Guggenheim branches, as well as the Hermitage Las Vegas, are noteworthy because, unlike the Guggenheim Bilbao, which was developed in partnership with the Basque government, they are partnerships with private-sector actors.

The Guggenheim's most recent undertakings, in Helsinki and Abu Dhabi, return to the original approach of partnering primarily with governments. In June 2015, the winning architectural design for the Guggenheim Helsinki was announced. However, that project has encountered a number of roadblocks. The first came shortly after the museum presented its initial proposal to the City of Helsinki in 2012. The skepticism with which this proposal was met led to the submission of a revised proposal in 2013, which included extensive changes to the financial model and the museum operating structure (SRG Foundation 2013). While some welcome the prospect of increased tourism that a Guggenheim might generate, others reject a model of Finnish taxpayer subsidization of an American initiative. The opposition has been so strong in some quarters that it spawned a parallel competition alongside the one launched by the city for the architectural contract. The "Next Helsinki" parallel competition invited proposals for alternative strategies for developing the cultural life of Helsinki. "Our competition—not really a competition at all, rather a call for ideas, an anti-competition—sought to ask first if a massive foreign museum was the highest and best use for public resources, especially in an aspirationally egalitarian social democracy like Finland."[4] Incensed that Helsinki might "surrender such a fabulous site to

[3.] For example, in early 2016, this space showed Jackson Pollock's mural, Energy Made Visible. The exhibition notes indicate that the painting is held by the University of Iowa Museum of Art and had recently undergone an 18-month cleaning and conservation process at the Getty in Los Angeles. The exhibition is curated by the Senior Consulting Curator from the Clyfford Still Museum in Denver. At the same time, the mural was commissioned by Peggy Guggenheim in 1943 and has recently been on view as part of her collection. <http://www.deutsche-bank-kunsthalle.de/kunsthalle/assets/presse/JP_Fact_sheet_EN.pdf>.

some starchitect supermarket," "the cultural equivalent of Starbucks,"[5] the initiative assembled an international jury and reviewed 217 proposals from 40 countries.

While the parallel competition arguably had more of a symbolic impact on the progress of Guggenheim efforts in Finland, in September 2016, the Finnish Government cut $45 million of funding for the museum as part of a larger austerity package. Many thought the project might be dead, however Guggenheim has since come back with a restructured funding package relying to a much greater degree on private contributions. The City of Helsinki will soon vote on this latest proposal.

The Hermitage

The Hermitage joined with the Guggenheim for the failed Las Vegas satellite. However, The Hermitage Amsterdam, opened in 2009, has been a success. The Hermitage did not initiate the satellite project in Amsterdam; instead, their Dutch colleagues approached them. Ties between the Russian and Dutch art communities were relatively close due to numerous art exchanges. Significant historical ties exist between the Netherlands and Russia and the Hermitage has the greatest collection of Dutch masters outside of the Netherlands.

Philanthropic support to the Russian state museum had previously been forthcoming from the Netherlands. In 1996, coinciding with a traveling exhibition from St. Petersburg on "Catherine the Great, the Emperor, and the Arts," a major fundraising campaign was held in the Netherlands to provide the Rembrandt Gallery in the Russian Hermitage with a new roof, daylight control, and lighting. Money from private individuals and organizations provided enough funding for three major restoration projects in St. Petersburg and provided the foundation for the Friends of the Hermitage that would later fund the Amsterdam branch.

Much of the impetus behind the Hermitage Amsterdam came from Ernst Veen, director of Amsterdam's De Nieuwe Kerk. He had a personal relationship with the Hermitage director, Mikhail Piotrovsky. He made the initial approach on behalf of the city of Amsterdam when a heritage building, centrally located on the Amstel River, became available and city leaders were looking for a creative use for it. Veen proposed a Hermitage branch,

[4] <http://www.nexthelsinki.org/#about>.
[5] Ibid.

which would both complement the city's already thriving art landscape and benefit from existing Dutch-Russian ties. Timing was propitious with the main fundraising for the Hermitage Amsterdam taking place just before the 2008 financial crisis. The initial Hermitage Amsterdam agreement specified that there would be no new Hermitage satellites in close European cities for a period of time. Veen did a press junket to Paris, Berlin, and other European cities in advance of the Hermitage Amsterdam opening. The message was that "Europe is getting a new museum."

Piotrovsky was receptive, partly because a satellite would create a welcome new revenue stream. "The museum was facing both a surplus of deferred maintenance projects and a lack of funds. Its new Dutch friends put sufficient funds at its disposal within an incredibly short time" (Tromp 2009:202). As Piotrovsky put it, "art is more important than money. But money is not unimportant" (Tromp 2009:202). The St. Petersburg Hermitage gets one euro per visitor to the Amsterdam branch (Tromp 2009:202). Operations ostensibly cost five million euros a year, with half coming from receipts and the other half through fund-raising (Tromp 2009:216). Hermitage Amsterdam operates more or less independently from St. Petersburg (Tromp 2009:203). The Amsterdam branch mostly shows art from the St. Petersburg storage and some exhibits from local Dutch museums.[6] When asked about the Hermitage "expansion" to Amsterdam, Piotrovsky took issue with the terminology. "Sure, but it's not about expansion, it's about access. We have extensive and marvellous collections. Here we can only show a small part of them" (Tromp 2009:201). The Hermitage ostensibly holds over 3 million objects in its collection. Approximately 65,000 of them are on display in the 350 galleries of the St. Petersburg museum (Russia Gallery).

There were some contributions from the city, the province and the state to get the Dutch museum up and running. But, there is no public money for Hermitage Amsterdam operations. There are several long-term sponsorships from corporate donors, like Phillips and Heineken. This sort of activity contributes to their corporate social responsibility mission and they benefit from the fact that they can use the museum building a few times a year for their events.

Guggenheim and Louvre—Saadiyat Island

Saadiyat Island is a development project of the Government of Abu Dhabi under the auspices of the Tourism Development and Investment Company

[6] For example, in the summer of 2015, the two exhibits were "Alexander, Napoleon, and Josephine," from St. Petersburg, and a portrait exhibit from the Rijksmuseum.

(TDIC). The cultural district is one part of a larger development that includes a business district, residences, beach resorts, marinas, golf courses, schools, and universities. It is just one component of a far-reaching urban planning vision, called Plan Abu Dhabi 2030. The Saadiyat Island cultural district will be an "iconic precinct" (Abu Dhabi UPC 2013:11) in the capital city, featuring three museums: the Guggenheim Abu Dhabi, the Louvre Abu Dhabi, and the Sheikh Zayed Museum, named for the founding President of the United Arab Emirates, and focusing on the history and traditions of the UAE. None of these museums has formally opened. The Louvre was originally scheduled to open in 2012, however that has been pushed back to 2017. The Jean Nouvel building is complete and an inaugural director was appointed in late 2016. Guggenheim construction is yet to begin. In the meantime, events are being held to create buzz and anticipation about the eventual openings, including public lectures by the architects and sample exhibitions in Abu Dhabi and elsewhere.

The Louvre Abu Dhabi was established as a result of an agreement signed between the Government of France and the Government of Abu Dhabi in 2007. The Louvre Abu Dhabi is not intended to be "an outpost" of the Paris museum. They will collaborate, but the Abu Dhabi Louvre will ostensibly build a permanent collection that contains more twentieth century art than its French cousin (Future 2012). For the Guggenheim, the "Tourism Development and Investment Company (TDIC), an independent company of ADTA, will own the museum, while the Guggenheim Foundation will create and manage the museum's programs including collection development, exhibitions, and educational projects" (Thompson 2008:23).

Saadiyat Island is just one piece of a much larger story of Gulf state participation in art markets (McClellan 2012). The Qatari royal family has become a major player. In recent years, it has broken records by purchasing art works for hitherto unseen prices. (Paul Cézanne's *The Card Players* for $250 million in 2011; Paul Gauguin's *When Will You Marry* for $300 million in 2015). They have also supported other initiatives, like a large-scale sculpture by Richard Serra in the Qatari desert and built the Museum of Islamic Art, designed by I.M. Pei. Sharjah, another Emirate, hosts a thriving gallery scene and a biennial. It was also named the cultural capital of the Arab world by UNESCO in 1998.

Why have museums opened satellite branches?

As the previous section suggests, the various stakeholders in museum satellites have different motivations. This is especially true for the public and private sector partners. A number of factors seem to be driving this strategy for museums. In some cases, museums are experiencing a reduction in funding or are confronting a need to enhance their funding to finance their operations. The Guggenheim was in poor financial shape when Thomas Krens sought out international partners to serve as satellite locations. To a certain degree, the Hermitage was also looking for new sources of revenue when it agreed to establish an outpost in Amsterdam. In all cases, they can leverage their "inventory"—their extensive collections in storage—to create new streams of revenue. The Louvre was entirely funded by the French government until 1993. Since then, the government only provides 70 percent of its needs (Ajana 2015:322). So, it, too, can benefit from new revenue streams. Travelling exhibits have offset some costs. For example, loans from the Louvre to the High Museum in Atlanta reportedly netted the Paris museum $6.4 million to use for gallery restoration (Maher 2007). When the Hermitage takes an exhibition abroad, it typically asks for one or one and a half million dollars (Tromp 2009:202). This suggests that satellites are the next natural step in an already transnational projection of its collections, partially to augment funds.

The governments who partner with museums have multiple motives that are both material and ideational. In several instances, the city or region perceives a need or an opportunity to stimulate its economy. They see the museum as a magnet or an anchor that can attract tourists and also generate jobs in the museum itself and in cognate services. Bilbao is the obvious example of such a strategy. "Supported by the governing conservative Basque Nationalist Party (PNV) and publicly financed to the tune of $150 million by various levels of government in the Autonomous Community of the Basque Country, the Guggenheim Bilbao is the product less of cultural policy than of economic policy" (Fraser 2005:47).

Saadiyat Island is an economic stimulus strategy of a different sort. Whereas Bilbao sought to reinvigorate a declining, deindustrialized region, Saadiyat Island is the centerpiece of a new economic development project that is being created from scratch on an island off Abu Dhabi. Abu Dhabi is extremely rich. At the same time, there is benefit to be derived from enhancing this wealth and diversifying its economy away from oil and toward tourism (Thompson 2008:22; HRW 2009). The appeal of increased tourism and possible accompanying job creation also resonated in Amsterdam, Helsinki, and Las Vegas.

In addition to the commercial prospects, numerous other motivations are in play when governments partner with museums. For example, related to the desire for economic stimulus is an effort at (re)branding. In order to build a brand, there must be a narrative, ideally of distinctiveness, which is then disseminated through "brand channels," like the media (Plaza et al. 2013). Bilbao clearly sought to fashion a different identity that would distance it from declining industries and terrorist presence. Abu Dhabi is arguably seeking through its development of the cultural district on Saadiyat Island to "reshape the 'image' of the Arab world" so that it includes "world-class" cultural hubs (Ajana 2015:316). Verena Formanek, senior project manager for the Abu Dhabi Guggenheim, said "Most of the people visiting us today don't know the difference between Dubai and Abu Dhabi, so we needed to work with the Guggenheim brand. No one in the world would have looked at Abu Dhabi without that name" (quoted in Batty 2012). The Abu Dhabi Tourism Authority describes Saadiyat Island as "a destination everyone in the world of art and culture would have to visit, annually and more than once, by building a series of permanent institutions—museums, performing art centers, exhibition halls, educational institutions in the arts—that through its collections, architecture and programs will become one of the greatest concentrations of cultural experience anywhere in the world" (cited in Thompson 2008:23). Las Vegas sought to rebrand itself, through the museum satellites as well as high end retailers and top-chef restaurants, as a destination for tourists who may not be attracted by the gaming industry. In Amsterdam and Helsinki, supporters have invoked a version of the branding motivation, suggesting that the arrival of a Hermitage or Guggenheim could reinforce or augment their brands as European cultural centers. The Bilbao experience suggests that allying with a globally recognized museum can allow a place to establish an international reputation quickly (Ajana 2015:317), however others have noted that this was as much about Bilbao as it was about the Guggenheim—a unique constellation of factors came together in that place at that time to create the outcomes that Bilbao experienced (Bathurst 2014).

In addition to these elements, we might also point to the opportunity for art partnerships to create opportunities for dialogue. "Equally important to the rationales of these projects is the desire to create a bridge between Western and Arabic art and a platform for retelling the histories and stories of the region, some of which have remained undocumented so far" (Ajana 2015:316). Even Helsinki is being sold in this way. In the Guggenheim's recent revised proposal to the City of Helsinki, they write, "Residents of Finland and international visitors alike would become active participants in the exchange of relevant contemporary ideas within an expanding global arts community" (SRG Foundation 2013:10). It further notes that, "Finland serves as an active bridge between East and West and is located at the nexus of the Nordic and Baltic regions" (SRG Foundation 2013:13).

The foregoing begs the question, why do corporations get involved in some of these arrangements? The Deutsche Bank provides perhaps the greatest insight because they partnered with Guggenheim for the Berlin location. Outside of the relationship with Guggenheim, Deutsche Bank has identified the promotion of art as a component of its corporate philanthropy. This sort of corporate social responsibility practice can burnish the bank brand and provide it with an opportunity to forge a distinctive corporate social responsibility policy. Beyond its partnership with the Guggenheim, Deutsche Bank oversees Art Works, its "global art program." The bank has its own collection of art, some of which it exhibits on its premises. It supports a myriad of projects, including an "Artist of the Year" award and a magazine about art, ostensibly making are more widely accessible. Ultimately, then, the various actors who participate in the transnationalization of the museum do so for their own political, economic, and cultural reasons.[7]

The Museum—What kind of transnational actor?

The seeds of the current conversation about transnational actors date to the early 1970s when scholars like Keohane and Nye questioned the state centric nature of the international system (Jönsson 2010, 23). They saw greater complexity of as well as significant activity by non-state actors. Early versions of this debate asked whether increased influence by transnational actors translated into declining influence for the state. Attention returned to transnational actors again in the 1990s with a spate of scholarship on globalization, transnational advocacy networks, and epistemic communities (see Risse 2002 for a review of this second wave).

Contemporary definitions include the following: transnational actors "operate on a cross-border basis, pursue the same set of goals everywhere, and address a global audience. This does not mean that their national affiliates, subsidiaries, or chapters have no autonomy: but they possess a clear overall image and exist as international, often legal entities, whether as church, corporation, or federation" (Josselin and Wallace 2001:3). The term, transnational, "refers to actors, interactions and flows that cross conventional borders, go beyond established patterns, and can be seen as an alternative to state-centric perspectives" (Jönsson 2010:40). These definitions seem able to accommodate the museum as a transnational actor, but what kind?

---

[7] <DeutscheBank website http://art.db.com/en/concept.html>.

128

There is no authoritative typology of transnational actors (Jönsson 2010:31). Yet there are some standard categories in the IR literature. Risse (2002:256) distinguishes transnational actors along two dimensions: their internal structure and their motivations. Internal structure captures whether the actor is a formal organization or a looser network (Risse 2002:256). In Risse's formulation, motivations can be instrumental, focused on the interests of the organization itself, or geared toward the common good or principled advocacy (2002:257). This emphasis on motivation is echoed elsewhere in the literature. "A distinction is commonly made between for-profit and non-profit organizations, between firms and so-called non-governmental organizations (NGOs)" (Jönsson 2010:31; see also Higgott, Underhill and Bieler 2000:1 and Downie 2013). This dichotomy has been expanded and rendered more complex. But, these basic categories provide a good starting point for situating museums in the conversation about transnational actors.

For-profit transnational actors

There is no doubt that satellites have evoked for many the corporatization or the commercialization of the museum in a way that invites comparisons to the multinational corporation (MNC). For example, Guggenheim Bilbao has been described as "the museum idea dreamed up by Krens to make the Guggenheim an international corporation interested in questions of growth and expansion, as well as stimulating business in the visual arts" (Guasch and Zulaika 2005:17). Krens has been both lauded and criticized for "his appropriation of for-profit business models, aggressive globalizing through an international network of branch museums, ties to corporations, deals with foreign governments, and exhibitions featuring luxury consumer products" (Fraser 2005:56). Much of the terminology used to discuss the Guggenheim evokes transnational business, including reference to the "Guggenheim Consortium" (Guasch and Zulaika 2005:16) and satellites as franchises.

In some instances, the Guggenheim itself makes the connection to MNCs. Peter Lewis, the president of the Solomon R. Guggenheim Foundation, has called the Foundation "the parent corporation of the Guggenheim Bilbao." Much has been made of the fact that Krens has a master's degree in studio art and a master's degree in business from the Yale School of Management (Fraser 2005:55; Haacke 2005:114). And, of course, not only for the Guggenheim, but for all of the museums involved, raising revenue is a key objective.

More recently, the commercial dimensions of the Abu Dhabi initiative have also been criticized, implicating not only Guggenheim, but also the Louvre.

Philippe Regnier, the editor of *Journal Des Arts*, claims that a museum is—or should be—distinct from a commercial or corporate enterprise (in Maher 2007): "The only really troubling thing in this project is that Abu Dhabi was determined to acquire a [desirable] name—in this case that of the Louvre, the name of the most prestigious museum in the world—and France sold the name of the Louvre like one might sell the name of a shoe store, or a store for ready-to-wear clothes. In other words, like a brand name [...] And with that, you get into a whole new view [of museums] that is no longer simply artistic but is also very much commercial."

What other attributes do museum satellites share with MNCs? MNCs expand their reach across borders; they create subsidiaries and franchises; they strike deals with governments. The deal between the French and Abu Dhabi governments creates a 30-year arrangement during which time the Abu Dhabi museum has essentially bought rights to the Louvre name. The deal also gives the Abu Dhabi museum access to advice from a consortium of 12 French cultural entities, assembled under the title Agence France-Muséums, as well as a commitment to organize joint exhibitions. In return, the Louvre reportedly earns $1.26 billion (Economist), $525 million for use of the name alone (Maher 2007). At the same time, the Louvre Abi Dhabi is not a branch of the Louvre Paris. The branch and its permanent collection are owned by the Government of Abu Dhabi. A similar arrangement exists for the Guggenheim. It will be involved in the programming and guide acquisitions, but Abu Dhabi will own the building and acquire its own permanent collection (Brake 2006). All of this money changing hands in exchange for consulting services and licensing rights resembles MNC activity.

Museum satellites, like most modern museums, have a strong consumer orientation, leading one commentator to suggest that they are transforming "from public educational institutions into corporate entertainment complexes..." (Fraser 2005:42). Popular culture exhibits, like the Guggenheim's The Art of the Motorcycle and Armani, have a wider attraction (Fraser 2005:50). Museum gift shops and restaurants can also make the museum a consumer destination that does not require a visit to the art collection. Just as the cities and regions that partner with museums are often concerned about their brand, so do the museums themselves engage in image or brand control, reminding us of MNCs. Fraser (2005:46) argues that "the museum is aggressive in policing its image and has threatened unauthorized reproductions with legal proceedings. When a local artist who runs a pasta shop started selling dry macaroni in the shape of Gehry's building, the response from museum lawyers was swift and unequivocal: cease production of the noodle or prepare to be sued."

The commercial aspects of MNCs are not the only attributes that resonate in a conversation about museum satellites. Just as Walmart, Starbucks, and McDonalds have been criticized for offering a cookie cutter product that is identical in every incarnation and that threatens to homogenize the broader landscape in their respective sectors, so does the Guggenheim especially come in for criticism as a cultural imperialist force. Not just the commercialization of art, which the Louvre Abu Dhabi also arguably represents, but the projection of a museum model that threatens the socio-cultural distinctiveness of the communities where they locate, is part of the concern raised especially about Guggenheim hewing too closely to MNC practices.

Furthermore, the Guggenheim and the Louvre have been embroiled in controversy about worker's conditions in the Emirates. In many ways, it evokes the campaign aimed at MNCs to stop using sweatshop labour. In 2009, Human Rights Watch published a report entitled, "The Island of Happiness': Exploitation of Migrant Workers on Saadiyat Island, Abu Dhabi." The report chronicles worker abuse in the construction projects, notably "employee-paid recruiting fees; visas controlled by employers; very low wages often far below what was promised workers in their home countries; and restrictions on organizing and no real access to legal remedies" (HRW 2009:1). These conditions are in addition to long hours in extreme heat. Many of these practices are apparently illegal in the Emirates, yet the laws are not enforced (HRW 2009:2). The organization called upon the Guggenheim and Louvre foundations, New York University, and the international architectural firms active in Abu Dhabi to obtain contractual guarantees from their partners responsible for constructing their facilities in Abu Dhabi to uphold worker rights (HRW 2009:9).

All of this seems quite persuasive in underlining the similarities between MNCs and museums. Still, we must stop short of saying that the museum *is* now an MNC. Museums are not earning money for their shareholders, but rather to fund operations. Museums retain a distinct mission to conserve and exhibit art and to educate the public about it. MNC-like attributes are on display across the museum sample to varying degrees, however perhaps the Guggenheim (and to a certain degree, the Louvre in Abu Dhabi) evokes the MNC more than the Hermitage. Museums are borrowing from the MNC playbook and noticing this is important. However, simply equating globally minded museums with MNCs forecloses an inquiry into many other aspects of the transnational museum's activity. Let us turn to the other familiar category, the NGO.

Non-Profit Transnational Actors

"If firms are private actors pursuing private profits, NGOs are private actors pursuing public purposes" (Jönsson 2010:31). Museums share some attributes of the NGO, but not others. The International Council of Museums (ICOM) defines a museum as "a non-profit, permanent institution in the service of society and its development, open to the public, which acquires, conserves, researches, communicates and exhibits the tangible and intangible heritage of humanity and its environment for the purposes of education, study, and enjoyment" (ICOM 2007). While NGOs are often associated with a principled cause, museums are not typically involved in advocacy and they do not typically seek to influence policy processes. One could argue that museum's raison d'être is itself a principled cause of sorts—arts preservation and education, as well as cross-cultural understanding. Indeed, the commercialization of the museum and its appropriation of MNC practices arguably diminishes this more principled mandate. In the absence of the satellite strategy, museums might more comfortably fit in the NGO transnational actor category.

Depending on the country, museums are non-governmental actors to varying degrees. The Guggenheim Foundation, for example is a private entity. The Louvre and the Hermitage, on the other hand, receive funding from their respective governments. It is worth noting that NGOs generally are not completely autonomous from the state (Higgott, Underhill and Bieler 2000:6). At a minimum, they exist along a spectrum (Josselin and Wallace 2001:2). Some are creations of the state; some are enlisted by states to do work on their behalf, which is also true of the museum.

A museum is like a foundation in some ways. However, foundations are more typically granting organizations that fund research, often relating to policy issues (Stone and Garnett 1998:4). A museum evokes some of the characteristics of an epistemic community in that it is a repository of expertise and can offer advice. Both the Guggenheim and the Louvre have been operating in this capacity with some controversy, offering advice to government partners, especially in Abu Dhabi, on art purchases. Nonetheless, it is actually an empirical question the degree to which there is a museum community characterized by "principled beliefs, ...shared causal beliefs, ...

shared notions of validity, ... and a common policy enterprise" (Haas 1992:3). These attributes suggest a cohesion across the museum community that is unproven. They may have more in common with "transnational communities" (Djelic and Quack 2010) than epistemic communities.

Even if we can identify those driving the museum satellite phenomenon as some sort of community, it tells us little about their objectives and effects. The same can be said of classing museum branches as public–private partnerships. "Partnerships can be understood as voluntary cooperative arrangements between actors from two or more societal spheres (state, market, civil society) with non-hierarchical decision-making procedures" (Jönsson 2010:36). The satellite museums are surely this, but this tells us little about the drivers, nature, and consequences of the partnerships. Museum branches are also surely part of a network. According to Jönsson (2010), networks are "informal constellations without official status....Networks represent a more horizontal, 'flat,' non-hierarchical mode of organization" (Jönsson 2010:39). "Networks represent more than fleeting encounters, but less than permanent institutions" (Jönsson 2010:39). The Guggenheim is, itself, a sort of network. Exhibitions can circulate among the various Guggenheim locations (SRG Foundation 2013:20). This tells us something about the flows and interdependencies, but again, little about the origins and substance of the links between the various nodes. Therefore, the museum is, by definition a non-profit entity, but it does not map perfectly onto any variant of the non-governmental organization.

Cultural diplomat

While not typically part of the transnational actor discussion, there is a fruitful overlap with the cultural diplomacy literature, which increasingly recognizes the contribution that non-state and private sector actors can make to cultural diplomacy. Many formulations of cultural diplomacy presume that governments are its key agents (Mark 2010). However, a shift in focus toward the preferred *outcome* of cultural diplomacy—greater mutual understanding—can accommodate non-governmental actors as cultural diplomats (Cummings 2003; Goff 2013, 2017; Schneider 2003). Some of the modern museum satellites situate their work in this way.[8]

Interestingly, the Guggenheim is not the first private museum that tried to develop international franchises. Nelson Rockefeller, a benefactor of the Museum of Modern Art (MoMA) in New York had for many years tried to open

---

[8] On museums as agents of cultural diplomacy, see Cai (2013), Grincheva (2013), and Nisbett (2013). On museums and cultural policy, see Jenkins (2005, 2014).

a series of MoMA franchises in several Brazilian cities, including São Paulo, Rio de Janeiro and Belo Horizonte (Guilbaut 2005). Indeed, Rockefeller was vying with the French at the time for this kind of cultural influence in Brazil. This effort was part of a Cold War fight against the spread of communism, founded on the idea that if Latin Americans embrace American art, they will also embrace the ideology that animates it (Guilbaut 2005). MoMA's goals in this endeavor were more political than economic as compared with contemporary museum branches. They were tools of cultural diplomacy.

Ernst Veen sees the Hermitage Amsterdam as having a cultural diplomacy dimension. "I am a product of the Cold War. Here and now I want to make a nice exhibition. But, at the same time I also want our institution to make a small contribution to open political relations between Russia and the Netherlands" (Tromp 2009:217). When asked why he did not choose to collaborate with the Louvre or the Met, which might be simpler, Veen says, "It arises from the choices we have been making for years as we have put together our exhibitions in De Nieuwe Kerk. Why do we do shows on Afghanistan, or on Morocco, or Turkey? It has to do with our wish to use art to say something more about other cultures. Hopefully, it helps people to understand each other better" (Tromp 2009:217). An entire room in the Hermitage Amsterdam, called The Russia Gallery, is dedicated to the origins of the museum against the backdrop of historical relations between the Netherlands and Russia. It traces "warm contacts" between the two nations from the time of Tsar Peter the Great in 1697. The establishment of a Hermitage satellite in Amsterdam is portrayed as the culmination or a natural outgrowth of centuries of positive ties. In this room, the Amsterdam museum is lightheartedly referred to as an "embassy" and an "ambassador" of Russia's national museum.

The Louvre Abu Dhabi aims to be the world's first universal museum, ranging across millennia and multiple societies, cultures, and civilizations. At a 2013 exhibit promoting the opening of the Louvre Abu Dhabi, HE Sheikh Sultan bin Tahnoon Al Nahyan, Chairman of Abu Dhabi Tourism & Culture Authority, said that, "even before opening its doors, Louvre Abu Dhabi is setting its precedent as a place of cross-cultural dialogue and exchange" ("Louvre" 2013). It is arguably not only exposure to the art that bridges cultures, promotes dialogue and understanding. For some, the business partnerships themselves contribute to this objective. As McClellan puts it (in Maher 2007): "the rhetoric you hear consistently around the openings of these [new] museums is that they will foster dialogue between east and west. And that's a very important justification for museums I think all over the world. And they're putting that into operation, in effect, by bridging the east and the west through this partnership." Supporters of the Helsinki Guggenheim also invoke a similar argument about the prospect of bridging difference and fostering dialogue.

Whether museums can effectively function as cultural diplomats is an empirical question for another study. Nonetheless, that museum satellites evoke aspects of cultural diplomacy complicates efforts to categorize them as transnational actors. It drives home the fact that museums do not fit easily into the standard categories that we use.

Conclusions

The satellite museum has emerged in recent years as a distinctive transnational actor. It straddles many of the standard categories in the field and bleeds into others that are not traditionally part of that conversation. Drawing on Risse's (2002) two dimensions, the *structure* of museum branches evokes both formal organizations and looser networks. In terms of *motivations*, museum satellites exhibit attributes of both for-profit and non-profit actors. Museum satellites are also unique transnational actors in terms of their purpose and influence. Transnational actor studies, including those devoted to activist networks and epistemic communities, often focus on direct policy impact. Indeed, Downie notes that the "principal question most scholars seek to answer" about transnational actors is, "under what conditions do transnational actors influence policy outcomes?" (Downie 2013:176). While museum satellites exhibit all the attributes of a transnational actor, they do not share this objective. Their impact can be quite significant—stimulating economic development; contributing in positive and negative ways to meaning-making, identity formation, and narratives about nationalism and place; shaping the physical landscape—but it is not typically a policy influence.

This preliminary analysis, then, delivers a clearer understanding of what museums *are not* as opposed to what they *are*. While a useful first step, it invites a shift away from an inquiry into what museums *are* toward what they *do*. What are the practices that define their activity? It is likely in subjecting specific examples of museum satellites to this kind of analysis that we can gain greater purchase on their unique brand of transnational activity. Future research should reflect this orientation.

References

Abu Dhabi Urban Planning Council (UPC). (2013) Plan Abu Dhabi 2030. <http://gsec.abudhabi.ae/Sites/GSEC/Navigation/EN/publications,did=90378>.

Ajana, Btihaj. (2015) Branding, Legitimation and the Power of Museums: The Case of the Louvre Abu Dhabi. *Museum & Society* (July) 13 (3): 316–335.

Azua, Jon. (2005) Guggenheim Bilbao: 'Coopetitive' Strategies for the New Culture-Economy Spaces. In *Learning from the Guggenheim Bilbao*, eds. Anna Maria Guasch and Joseba Zulaika, 73–95. Reno: Center for Basque Studies, University of Nevada.

Bathurst, Matilda. (2014) *Guggenheim Bilbao Lets its Collection Speak for Itself.* Apollo: The American Art Magazine, October.

Batty, David. (2012) Guggenheim Delay Raises Big Question: Is Abu Dhabi Ready for Modern Art?. *The Guardian*, April 17 <http://www.theguardian.com/world/2012/apr/17/abu-dhabi-guggenheim-delay-question>.

Brake, Alan G. (2006) Abu Dhabi Announces Its Own Gehry-designed Guggenheim. *Architectural Record* 194 (10): 17.

Cai, Yunci. (2013) The Art of Museum Diplomacy: The Singapore–France Cultural Collaboration in Perspective. *International Journal of Politics*, Culture and Society 26: 127–144.

Cummings, Milton. (2003) *Cultural Diplomacy and the United States Government: A Survey.* Washington, DC: Center for Arts and Culture.

Djelic, Marie-Laure, and Sigrid Quack. (2010) *Transnational Communities: Shaping Global Economic Governance.* Cambridge, UK: Cambridge University Press.

Downie, Christian. (2013) Transnational Actors: Nongovernmental Organizations, Civil Society and Individuals. In *Routledge Handbook of Environmental Politics*, ed. Paul G. Harris, 176–186. Florence, US: Routledge Press.

(2014) *The Louvre Comes to the Gulf: The Start of a Brand-new Culture Hub.* Economist, November 18.

Fraser, Andrea. (2005) Isn't This a Wonderful Place? A Tour of a Tour of the Guggenheim Bilbao. In *Learning from the Guggenheim Bilbao*, eds. Anna Maria Guasch and Joseba Zulaika, 37–58. Reno: Center for Basque Studies, University of Nevada.

Future Arts Venues of the Saadiyat Cultural District Abu Dhabi. (2012) *Gulf Art Guide: Contemporary Visual Arts in the Arabian Peninsula*. <http://gulfartguide.com/abu-dhabi-2/the-new-abu-dhabi-museums/>.

Goff, Patricia. (2013) Cultural Diplomacy. In *The Oxford Handbook of Modern Diplomacy*, eds. Andrew Cooper, Jorge Heine, and Ramesh Thakur, 419–435. Oxford University Press.

Goff, Patricia. (2017) *Cultural Diplomacy*. Oxford Bibliographies.

Grincheva, Natalia. (2013) Cultural Diplomacy 2.0: Challenges and Opportunities in Museum International Practices. *Museum and Society* 11 (1): 39–49.

Guasch, Anna Maria, and Joseba Zulaika. (2005) Learning from the Bilbao Guggenheim: The Museum as a Cultural Tool. In *Learning from the Guggenheim Bilbao*, eds. Anna Maria Guasch and Joseba Zulaika, 7–20. Reno: Center for Basque Studies, University of Nevada.

Guilbaut, Serge. (2005) Sleeping in Bilbao: The Guggenheim as a New Cultural Edsel?. In *Learning from the Guggenheim Bilbao*, eds. Anna Maria Guasch and Joseba Zulaika, 133–147. Reno: Center for Basque Studies, University of Nevada.

Haacke, Hans (2005) The Guggenheim Museum: A Business Plan. In *Learning from the Guggenheim Bilbao*, eds. Anna Maria Guasch and Joseba Zulaika, 113–123. Reno: Center for Basque Studies, University of Nevada.

Haas, Peter M. (1992) Introduction: Epistemic Communities and International Policy Coordination. *International Organization* 46 (1): 1–35.

Higgott, Richard A., Geoffrey R.D. Underhill, and Andreas Bieler. (2000) Introduction: Globalization and Non-State Actors. In *Non-State Actors and Authority in the Global System*, eds. Richard A. Higgott, Geoffrey R.D. Underhill, and Andreas Bieler, 1–12. London: Routledge Press.

Human Rights Watch. (2009) *"The Island of Happiness": Exploitation of Migrant Workers on Saadiyat Island, Abu Dhabi.* <https://www.hrw.org/report/2009/05/19/island-happiness/exploitation-migrant-workers-saadiyat-island-abu-dhabi>.

International Council of Museums. (2004) Code of Ethics for Museums. <http://icom.museum/professional-standards/code-of-ethics/2-museums-that-maintain-collections-hold-them-in-trust-for-the-benefit-of-society-and-its-developme/>

International Council of Museums. (2007) Museum Definition. <http://icom.museum/the-vision/museum-definition/>

Jenkins, Barbara. (2005) Toronto's Cultural Renaissance. Canadian Journal of Communication 30: 169–186.

Jenkins, Barbara. (2014) National Cultural Policy and the International Liberal Order. In *Negotiations in a Vacant Lot*, eds. Lynda Jessup, Erin Morton, and Kirsty Robinson, 114–129. Montreal, QC: McGill-Queen's University Press.

Jönsson, Christer. (2010) Capturing the Transnational: A Conceptual History. In *Transnational Actors in Global Governance*, eds. Jonas Tallberg and Christer Jönsson, 22–44. Basingstoke, UK: Palgrave MacMillan.

Josselin, Daphné, and William Wallace. (2001) Non-State Actors in World Politics: A Framework. In *Non-State Actors in World Politics*, eds. Daphné Josselin and William Wallace, 1–20. New York: Palgrave Press.

(2013) Louvre Abu Dhabi Exhibition, Birth of a Museum, to Open on Saadiyat Island in April. Business Intelligence Middle East, February 4. <http://www.bi-me.com/main.php?id=60859&t=1>.

MacCannell, Dean. (2005) The Fate of the Symbolic in Architecture for Tourism: Piranesi, Disney, Gehry. In *Learning from the Guggenheim Bilbao*, eds. Anna Maria Guasch and Joseba Zulaika, 21–36. Reno: Center for Basque Studies, University of Nevada.

Maher, Heather. (2007) World: Western Museums Make Controversial Move East. *Radio Free Europe Radio Liberty*. <http://ww w.rferl.org/content/article/1075167.html>.

Mark, Simon L. (2010) Rethinking Cultural Diplomacy: The Cultural Diplomacy of New Zealand, the Canadian Federation and Quebec. *Political Science* 62 (1): 62–83.

McClellan, A. (2012) Museum Expansion in the Twenty-First Century: Abu Dhabi. *Journal of Curatorial Studies* 1 (3): 271–293.

Nisbett, Melissa. (2013) New Perspectives on Instrumentalism: An Empirical Study of Cultural Diplomacy. *International Journal of Cultural Policy* 19 (5): 557–575.

Plaza, Beatriz, Pilar Gonzalez-Casimiro, Paz Moral-Zuazo, and Courtney Waldron. (2013) *Culture-Led City Brands as Economic Engines: Theory and Empirics*. Association of Cultural Economics Working Paper Series AWP-05-2013.

Risse, Thomas. (2002) Transnational Actors and World Politics. In *Handbook of International Relations*, eds. Walter Carlsnaes, Thomas Risse, and Beth Simmons, 256-274. London, UK: Sage Publications.

Schneider, Cynthia P. (2003) D*iplomacy that Works: 'Best Practices' in Cultural Diplomacy*. Cultural Diplomacy Research Series, Center for Arts and Culture. Washington, DC.

Solomon R. Guggenheim Foundation. (2013) Guggenheim Helsinki: Revised Proposal 2013. <http://www.guggenheimhki.fi/wp-content/uploads/2013/08/gHelsinki_web_ENG1.pdf>

Stone, Diane, and Mark Garnett. (1998) Introduction: Think Tanks, Policy Advice and Governance. In *Think Tanks Across Nations: A Comparative Approach*, 1–20. Manchester, UK: Manchester University Press.

Sylvester, Christine. (2009) *Art/Museums: International Relations Where You Least Expect It*. Boulder: Paradigm Publishers.

Thompson, Seth. (2008) Globalization, Economics and Museums: Saadiyat Island's Cultural District in Abu Dhabi, UAE. *International Journal of the Arts in Society* 3 (3): 21-26.

Tromp, Jan. (2009) The Inspiration Behind the Hermitage Amsterdam. In *Amstelhof Hermitage Amsterdam: From Nursing Home to Museum*, eds. Nelleke Noordervliet, Carina van Aartsen, Jan Tromp, and Hans Ibelings, 194-219. Amsterdam: Hermitage Amsterdam.

Zulaika, Joseba. (2005) Desiring Bilbao: The Krensification of the Museum and its Discontents. In *Learning from the Guggenheim Bilbao*, eds. Anna Maria Guasch and Joseba Zulaika, 149–170. Reno: Center for Basque Studies, University of Nevada.

Creating Museums:
An Interview

Abbie Chessler and J.P. Singh

Editor's Note: *The following is an interview between Editor J.P. Singh and architect Abbie Chessler, conducted on 5 September 2016. This transcription is an abridged version; it has been edited for length and clarity. Managing Editor transcribed and edited the interview. Listen to the audio on theartsjournal.net.*

J.P. Singh: How did you get into that line of work?

Abbie Chessler: I was an art school graduate and had to figure out how to pay the rent. I got into the museum field very serendipitously, very accidentally, which is how people in my generation in the museum world got into it.

JP: What was the serendipity?

AC: I worked a number of jobs after getting my fine arts degree. I was back home in Baltimore when the National Aquarium opened. They had more visitors than anybody imagined in their wildest dreams. The Aquarium folks came into the photo lab where I was working as an assistant, needing help with ideas to accommodate the crowds. They had ideas about what needed to be done but didn't know how to get there. A light bulb went off in my head: *I know how to do all of these things.* They hired me as a contractor to do a project and it was successful. As I began to pursue work as a freelancer people would ask what have you done and say *Oh, you must be good. We'll hire you.* It was the gumption to put it together and just start working. In 1989 we formed Quatrefoil Associates.

By focusing on museums, I really came to understand the critical role museums have for us culturally and educationally. Museums provide an important narrative for the human existence. Right now this point of time, pre-presidential election in the United States of America in 2016, I feel the work I do is so important because it helps people learn from history. *How do you not repeat the mistakes of the past?*

For example, the museum that we just opened up in Los Angeles in May, the Go For Broke Education Center, is the legacy project for an organization founded by Japanese-Americans World War II veterans. They and their families were forcibly interned in "relocation" camps. Their families were stripped of their constitutional rights and the young men were asked to fight in the war. Their slogan was "Go For Broke." *We're going to prove that we're true American citizens. We're going to fight for all the rights that our families have been denied.* When you unpack all of the issues that we call national insecurity, it mirrors what's going on today exactly. If I have a chance in the work Quatrefoil designs for museums to impact even a handful of people I consider that worthwhile.

JP: This idea of memory and heritage is very different from the patrimonial ideal that glorifies the culture. As the designer, how did you prepare yourself for that role?

AC: When I listen I try to listen for the emotion and the undertone in the answer too. In working with client organizations, they see that I'm a white American woman. If I go into a group of Japanese Americans to talk about their family's experience in the camps, I have to be very honest. I have to speak from my heart to communicate with people, and reach out to establish trust and friendship so we can really talk about the deep issues.

In the Spring of 2016 we completed a project in Albuquerque, New Mexico: The Indian Pueblo Cultural Center. It's a cultural museum that represents all 19 of New Mexico's Pueblos. Here I am again a white American woman from the east coast coming into Pueblo culture. I said to the folks straight up in our first meeting *I just want you to know that if we make a misstep, if we don't understand something, if we say something that's not correct, if we say or do something that's offensive please, please tell us immediately so that we learn and we understand.* The curator and I built a really lovely relationship and she said ask me anything. I learned so much about spiritual traditions, values, families – things that aren't shared with outsiders. Most of what we talked

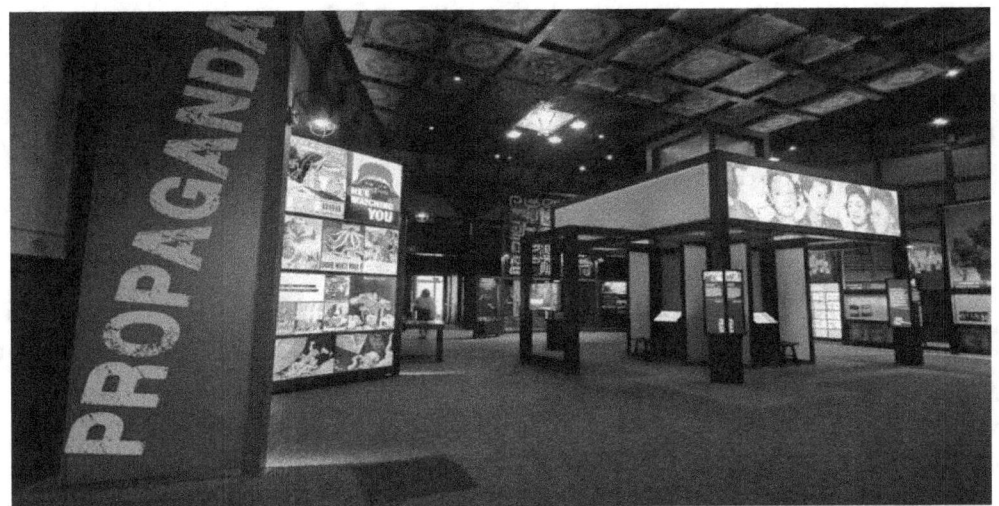

"Defining Courage" at the Go For Broke Education Center. *Image courtesy of Quatrefoil Associates.*

Scan here to watch Quatrefoil's video on the Go For Broke Education Center

http://bit.ly/2izS89c

Scan here to watch Quatrefoil's video on the Indian Pueblo Cultural Center

http://bit.ly/2hS3PYj

about isn't in the final exhibition but it helped us to develop a level of trust.

JP: Is openness and listening enough to build trust? How do you balance what you're hearing to what may be a comfortable design for them?

AC: I have a really talented staff. We do all these things as a team. We do workshops with the clients and ask a lot of questions. Then we start to put ideas on paper because we work in the design realm and a lot of it is visual. We start to feed back the ideas for the visitor experience so a client has something to check to see if we are understanding their messages. For me, the greatest reward is when a project opens and the people whose story we're telling say they're happy and they feel their story is being told. Then I feel it's a success.

There's no design ego. Nothing should ever look like a Quatrefoil design project because the design should reflect that cultural organization, that community. It's their story. It's not about us; it's about them.

JP: But I imagine it does look like a Quatrefoil design. That's why people come to you.

AC: They come to us for our process. We work with in-house curatorial teams, historians, community experts and technical advisors.

JP: What kind of research do you have to do? How do you organize the history you need to know before you walk in?

AC: We have a kick-off workshop with the client organization to bring consensus around a vision for the project and a mission. We talk a lot about what our goals are for the people who will visit. *What do we want them to say when they walk out? What do we want them to learn and feel from being here?* That gives us a framework. Once we have the framework, we can identify the stories that support these outcomes.

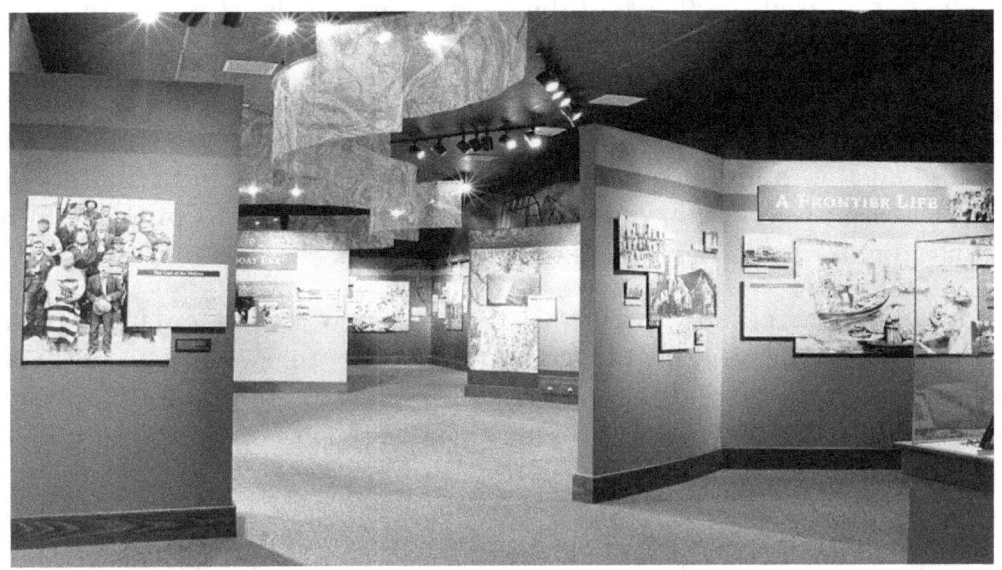

Delta Cultural Center. *Image courtesy of Quatrefoil Associates.*

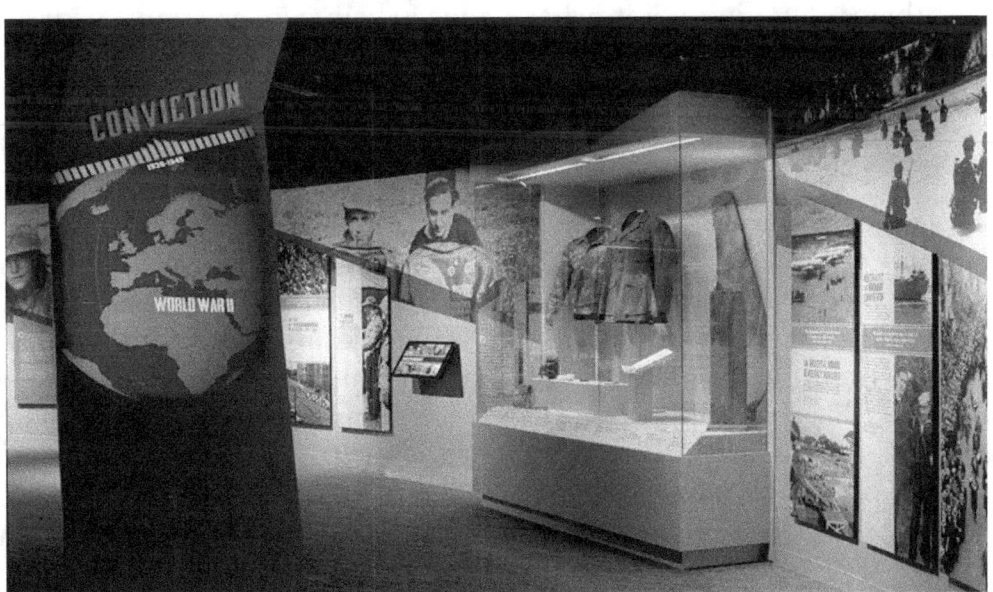

National Museum of American Jewish Military History. *Image courtesy of Quatrefoil Associates.*

JP: The design is all-inclusive of the design curation. That is already a very different way of thinking about the museum.

AC: It's not the grandma's attic of stuff anymore. That's not what people want to see and generally not what organizations want to put out there. Visitors to museums come with a varied set of expectations.

We are only tangentially involved with the new Smithsonian National Museum of African American History and Culture; that's going to be a very different museum. We're doing some media pieces and online stuff for them. It's all about stories and not just the past. They're bringing things right up to the Black Lives Matter movement in the exhibits.

We did something very similar in the Go For Broke exhibition where newsfeed is incorporated. One of the local ABC network affiliates is partnering with the Center to provide news updates. Coming up with approaches to keep content relevant and current in museums is a big part of the work we do.

JP: Is there a tipping-point where you've had conversations with the community and you feel comfortable? When do you say now I have some sense and I'm going to move forward?

AC: It's more of a process. There's so much minutiae that goes into designing a museum experience. We have regular meetings and conversations. The design team is pushing everybody along. We're pushing the rock up the hill together and having the difficult conversations. You see this finished thing that looks beautiful and effortless but it's like anything you see, dance or gymnastics, that looks effortless. There was a tremendous amount of effort that went into it that you don't see. If we do our job well the result is a powerful, memorable experience.

The Destruction of Memory

Tim Slade

Tim Slade's films have screened at more than 70 international film festivals. He has won a Gold Plaque at the Chicago HUGO Television Awards, and was nominated for awards at the Banff World Television Festival, the International Documentary Association Awards, and the Australian Film Institute Awards. Other documentary films include Blank Canvas *and* Musical Renegades. *He studied film at the College of Fine Arts, University of New South Wales.*

In 2010, I read Robert Bevan's *The Destruction of Memory: Architecture at War*. The book is an exploration of intentional cultural destruction and its use as a tool of warfare. Cultural destruction in this book becomes a type of war in its own right, in which the targets are buildings and monuments rather than an opposing army or enemy population. Bevan, an English heritage architect, writer and journalist, skillfully invests the book with urgency and revelation. Bevan draws out the crucial relationship between physical attacks on a people and simultaneous attacks on their cultural identity, as part of a concerted attempt by the perpetrator to erase the group's trace and singular presence.

Historical events such as the Taliban's destruction of the Buddhas of Bamiyan in 2001, the horrors of Kristallnacht and the fate of Carthage were known to me. But I did not know the extent to which the dynamics of this pervasive and deliberate process receded into the fog of war and conflict. Often seeming or being passed off as collateral damage, cultural destruction is an insidious process in which history, present, and future of a people can be effectively erased. People are more than their human form. Their cultural artefacts – their books, their buildings, their monuments, are where their collective identity is stored. When they are destroyed, so is this identity.

I embarked on adapting Bevan's book as a documentary in mid 2010, and the completed film was released in 2016 at a time when tragic ongoing events in Syria, Iraq and elsewhere gave the message of Robert Bevan's book and the film an extra urgency. Despite humanity's attempts to preserve its heritage, Bevan's message remains important: the general public as well as politicians, military personnel, lawyers and policy makers ¬– need to continue to hear it.

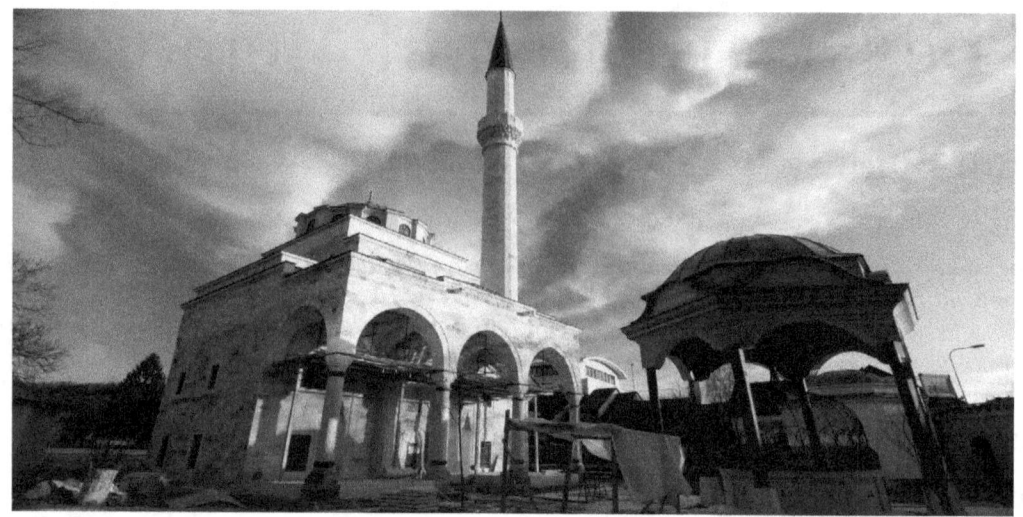

Rebuilding of Ferhadija Mosque, Banja Luka, Bosnia & Herzegovina. *Image: Derek Wiesehahn, Copyright 2016 Vast Productions USA*

What struck me most in the book, and would become the backbone of the film, was the way in which the international community responded to the issue, or more tellingly, didn't respond to the issue. The international community here includes states, international organizations, and transnational civil society. As a filmmaker, I felt that the ways in which laws and policy moved in or out of step with the destruction itself was a crucial part of the narrative.

There are few really compelling examples of a response to cultural heritage crimes. These include the jailing of two senior naval officials for their roles in the now infamous shelling of Dubrovnik's old town in December 1991, and the 27 September 2016 ruling at the International Criminal Court (ICC) that found Ahmad Al Faqi Al Mahdi guilty of crimes against humanity for the destruction of the Timbuktu mosques in June-July 2012. The latter ruling, recognising that destruction of cultural heritage is a crime against humanity, speaks eloquently, even if tragically, to Robert Bevan's thesis.

My film examines the history and the lack of urgency in humanity's efforts to curtail cultural destruction. To understand this, and to forge the possibility of better protection and response in the future, the film would have to first look to the slow but gradual efforts internationally to protect our cultural heritage.

The 1863 Lieber Code, commissioned by Abraham Lincoln, is an interesting early instance of legislation to protect heritage. The Code arose from the ashes of property targeted by enemy combatants in the ongoing U.S. Civil War and was the first piece of legislation to call for the protection of cultural property during armed conflict (Note 1). The first true universal exploration came in the 1899 and 1907 Hague Conventions, which declared forbidden 'to destroy or seize the enemy's property, unless such destruction or seizure be imperatively demanded by the necessities of war'.

The international community was responding primarily to the increased efficacy of the tools of warfare, including the advent of dirigibles, airplanes and advanced naval technology.

In 1933, Raphael Lemkin, a young Polish Jewish lawyer, prepared to present a paper to a League of Nations conference in Madrid. Inspired by the lack of action taken against aggressor states after World War I, Lemkin put forward a plan to create formalized international laws to prosecute 'barbarism', the systematic killing of particular ethnic or religious groups, and 'vandalism', the destruction of the cultural property and built environment of the targeted group. Lemkin saw the two modes of destruction as parallel processes that intended to erase a racial or ethnic group as well as their cultural imprints in architecture, iconography and dissemination of ideas.

Lemkin served in the Polish Army during the 1939 siege of Warsaw, later escaping to the United States, but the loss of several family members in the Holocaust as well as the targeted destruction of his own Polish Jewish cultural patrimony compelled him to write: *"It takes centuries and sometimes thousands of years to create a natural culture, but Genocide can destroy a culture instantly, like fire can destroy a building in an hour."* (Note 2)

Lemkin's proposal fell on deaf ears at the League of Nations, but its successor organization, the United Nations, created in the wake of World War II and the Holocaust, responded to Lemkin's appeals by creating an international convention to prevent and prosecute genocide. However, the 'cultural genocide' clauses of Lemkin's initial drafts were excised, partly due to the lobbying of nation states whose colonised Indigenous communities and their cultures had been victims of these processes.

Nevertheless, in late 1945, the United Nations Educational, Scientific and Cultural Organizations (UNESCO) was formed to 'respond to the firm belief of nations' that 'peace must be established on the basis of humanity's moral and intellectual solidarity' (Note 3). In 1954, the Hague Convention for the Protection of Cultural Property in the Event of Armed Conflict was crafted and signed by member states of UNESCO. Some states immediately ratified the Convention. Other key nations, such as the United Kingdom have yet to ratify it, although such a bill is being debated by Parliament that could become UK law early in 2017 (Note 4). The convention's subsequent two Protocols give further protections, the Second Protocol (1999) going some way in closing the military necessity loophole that has arguably limited the efficacy of the Convention.

In 1993, the UN Security Council established the International Criminal Tribunal for the former Yugoslavia (ICTY). It has its own rules and regulations specific to the Balkan context, which recognised the need to tackle the extensive cultural heritage crimes perpetrated during the Balkan Wars. The way the Tribunal would approach these crimes would draw on existing frameworks such as the 1954 Hague Convention. However, the military necessity argument limited the extent to which some seemingly clear cut targeted attacks, such as the shelling of the Mostar Bridge in November 1993 by Croat forces, were treated at the tribunal.

Importantly, the judgment in the Krstic case, examining the killing of Srebrenica's Bosnian Muslims and the parallel destruction of their mosques, stated that *"where there is physical or biological destruction there are often simultaneous attacks on the cultural and religious property of the targeted group as well, attacks which may be considered as evidence of an intent to physically destroy the group."* (Note 5)

Despite such important recognitions, there has been a lack of consensus at the Tribunal on how to view such crimes. In April 2015, appeal judges in the Tolimir case ruled that the trial judges had *'committed a legal error in considering the destruction of mosques'* (Note 6). The appeal judges determined that targeted cultural destruction cannot be considered as evidence of genocide, nor possibly even intent of genocide, noting that 'cultural genocide' had been discluded from the scope of the Genocide Convention.

Despite these contradictions, the overall work of the court, and of individuals like András Riedlmayer, has been vital to the success of such prosecutions. Riedlmeyer is bibliographer at the Aga Khan Fine Arts Library at Harvard University. He meticulously collected evidence in Kosovo and Bosnia in the aftermath of hostilities and served as an expert witness in several ICTY cases. Riedlmayer's work has set an informal standard for some cultural heritage workers collecting and documenting evidence of possible cultural crimes in recent and ongoing contexts.

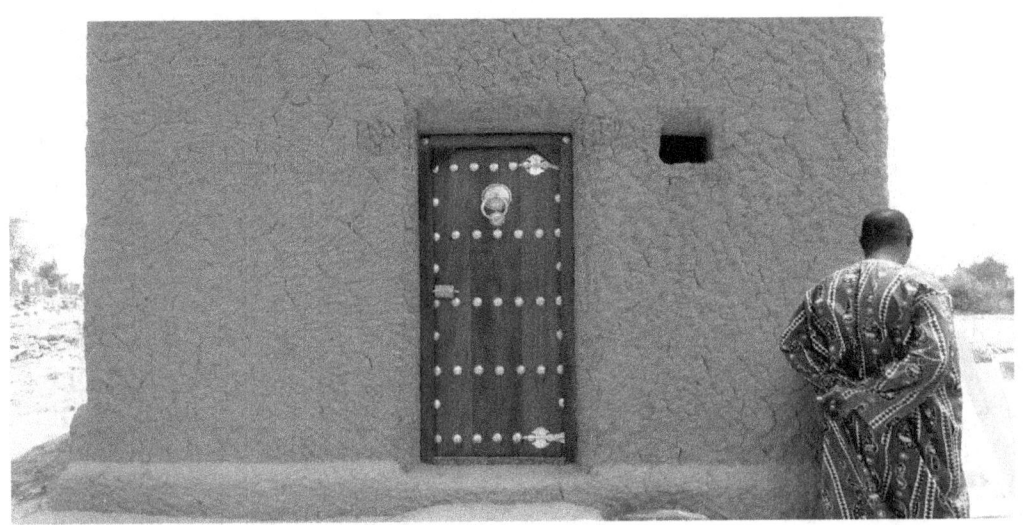

Reconstructed mausoleum, Timbuktu, Mali. *Image: Francois Rihouay, © 2016 Vast Productions USA*

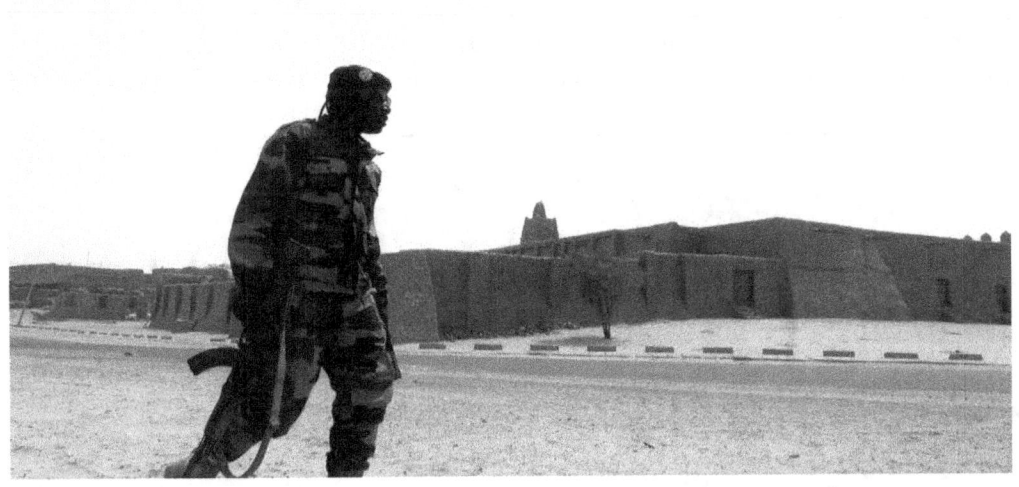

Professor Hamidovic in front of the Mostar Bridge, Bosnia & Herzegovina
Image: Faris Dobraca, © 2016 Vast Productions USA

The ICC is governed by the Rome Statute, which was adopted in 1998 and entered into force in 2002. Under Article 8 of the statute, War Crimes explicitly include *'Intentionally directing attacks against buildings dedicated to religion, education, art, science or charitable purposes, historic monuments, hospitals… provided they are not military objectives'* (Note 7). The court's then newly appointed Chief Prosecutor, Fatou Bensouda, made an immediate public reference to this provision when Islamic mausoleums were intentionally destroyed in Timbuktu, Mali in July 2012, warning the perpetrators, allegedly members of extremist group Ansar Dine, that their actions could constitute war crimes. The Prosecutor's office, at the request of the Malian government, began preliminary investigations and subsequently opened a case looking into various alleged crimes perpetrated in northern Mali.

In September 2015, Malian authorities arrested Ansar Dine member Ahmad Al Faqi Al Mahdi and handed him over to the court. His trial took place in late August 2016, and at its opening, Al Mahdi admitted guilt as to the war crime of intentionally directing attacks against historic monuments and buildings dedicated to religion, including nine mausoleums and one mosque in Timbuktu.

The prosecution's evidence was substantial – part of the highly public style of destruction favored by Da'esh, Ansar Dine and other extremist groups. The prosecution presented plentiful and incriminating video and photographic evidence of these acts of cultural destruction before the international court.

Al Mahdi expressed remorse and publicly disavowed the ideological frameworks that persuaded him to take part in the destruction. His admitted

---

Scan here to watch the *Destruction of Memory* trailer

https://vimeo.com/143061688

culpability presumably influenced sentencing; he received a term of 9 years after the prosection asked for 9 to 11 years.

What will be the short and long term impacts of this prosecution? Will other extremists see this as a deterrent? Will generals or political leaders be further cautioned?

In October 2016, Burundi and South Africa announced their intention to withdraw from the ICC. The nations argued that the court's focus was unfairly weighted towards prosecuting crimes in African states. But, the response from observers including journalists and human rights experts is that impunity for sitting heads of states and governments is a key factor in the desire to leave the court (Note 8).

There should never be impunity for crimes against culture. The UN member states, international courts and governments must unite to ensure that destruction – whether wanton, disproportionate, or explicitly willful – is not swept under the carpet of political convenience.

But there are glimmers of hope for the future legal persecution of attempts to erase people and their collective identity and memory. Experts in international cultural heritage and rights, including Professor Patty Gerstenblith as well as Professor Karima Bennoune, the UN Special Rapporteur in the field of cultural rights, are passionately encouraging awareness and writing about how such frameworks could be crafted.

In 2015, Justice Trindade made direct references to Raphael Lemkin's thwarted efforts in an International Court of Justice dissenting opinion. Rather than simply accepting the current language of the Convention as the appeal judges had done in the Tolimir case at the ICTY, Justice Trindade wrote: 'The (Genocide) Convention, essentially *people-centered*, will have a future if attention is rightly turned to its *rationale*, to its object and purpose... Already for some time, attention has been drawn to the shortcomings of the Convention against Genocide as originally conceived, namely: a) the narrowing of its scope, excluding cultural genocide...' (Note 9)

It is an enormous satisfaction to a filmmaker that the source author feels the adaptation has worked. Robert Bevan has written of the film that he may personally have made something more 'jagged' and 'pugnaciously dramatic', but that 'Tim has instead, created an effective call to peace rather than arms that, though passionate, appeals to our intellect more than our anger. It works... It is Tim's great skill that this central message comes through loud and clear: attacks on architectural heritage are not just an evidential "mark" of a genocidal project but can be an effective mechanism of carrying out this crime of crimes (genocide).' (Note 10)

Making the film, and delving into the history and present of cultural destruction, made clear for me the belief that there must be a concerted, sustained effort by the international community to address the issue and to assert the connection between cultural and human rights. I urge policy and decision makers to continue to create effective legal tools to bring justice to those whose identity and integrity are threatened by these acts, and I urge cultural heritage professionals to continue their brave, necessary work. Our past, and our future, depends on it.

Author's note: *I would like to acknowledge ideas contained in the book* The Destruction of Memory: Architecture at War *by Robert Bevan, and conversations with interviewees during the creation of the film* The Destruction of Memory, *in the writing of this article.*

Notes

1. Sourced from website for the U.S. Committee of the Blue Shield. http://uscbs.org/laws---treaties-1863-1977.html

2. Raphael Lemkin, The Evolution of the Genocide Convention, Lemkin Papers. New York Public Library, as quoted in Robert Bevan, *The Destruction of Memory: Architecture at War* (2006, Reaktion Books, London).

3. Sourced from UNESCO website http://en.unesco.org/about-us/introducing-unesco

4. Stone, Peter. (2016) Why ratifying the Hague Convention matters. The *Art Newspaper*, November 29 <http://theartnewspaper.com/comment/comment/why-ratifying-the-hague-convention-matters-/>

5. ICTY Trial IT-98-33-T (Prosecutor v. Radislav Krstic), Judgement, 2 August 2001.

6. ICTY Appeal Judgement Summary for Zdravko Tolimir, 8 April 2015.

7. ICC Rome Statute, Article 8 (b)(ix)

8. Simwaka, Fletcher. (2016) Africa's Retreat from the International Criminal Court is about impunity, not dignity. *The Washington Post*, November 8. <https://www.washingtonpost.com/news/global-opinions/wp/2016/11/08/africas-retreat-from-international-criminal-court-is-about-impunity-not-dignity/>

9. ICJ, Dissenting Opinion of Judge A.A. Cancado Trindade, Application of the Convention on the Prevention and Punishment of the Crime of Genocide (Croatia v. Serbia) 3 February 2015, Clause 520.

10. Robert Bevan, Milano Design Film Festival 2016 catalogue, introduction to 'The Destruction of Memory' film.

www.ingramcontent.com/pod-product-compliance
Lightning Source LLC
Chambersburg PA
CBHW081259170526
45165CB00011B/3346

* 9 7 8 1 6 3 3 9 1 5 1 1 4 *